THE FIRST HIGHLANDER

The First Highlander

Major-General David Stewart of Garth CB

Author of
*Sketches of the Character, Manners, and Present State
of the Highlanders of Scotland, with Details of the
Military Service of the Highland Regiments*

James Irvine Robertson

TUCKWELL PRESS

First published in Great Britain in 1998 by
Tuckwell Press
The Mill House
Phantassie
East Linton
East Lothian EH40 3DG
Scotland

Copyright © James Irvine Robertson, 1998

ISBN 1 86232 050 0

The publishers acknowledge subsidy from the Scottish Arts
Council towards the publication of this volume

British Library Cataloguing in Publication Data
A catalogue record for this book is available on request from the
British Library

The right of James Irvine Robertson to be identified as the
author of this work has been asserted by him in accordance with
the Copyright, Design and Patent Act 1988

Typeset by Carnegie Publishing, Chatsworth Rd, Lancaster
Printed and bound by Cromwell Press, Trowbridge, Wiltshire

Contents

	Illustrations	vi
	Acknowledgements	vii
	Foreword	1
1	Roots	5
2	To be a Soldier	14
3	Campaigns in the West Indies	22
4	Jungle Warfare	29
5	A Hero of Alexandria	36
6	Maida	48
7	Career in Suspense	58
8	Unemployment	66
9	Tartan	73
10	Genesis of the *Sketches*	82
11	Sword to Ploughshare	91
12	Just and Honourable Arrangement	101
13	Spurious Relations	107
14	Changes on the Estates	114
15	The *Sketches*	124
16	The King's Jaunt	134
17	God bless the Land of Cakes!	141
18	Fame but no Fortune	150
19	A Country Gentleman	156
20	Jobs and Money	164
21	Governor of St Lucia	170
22	The Dying Days of Slavery	176
23	Aftermath	182
	Sources	189
	Index	195

Illustrations

1. Colonel David Stewart of Garth CB.
2. Caricature of Stewart by Caroline Norton.
3. John Stewart of Garth.
4. Jessie Stewart of Garth.
5. Stewart's medals.
6. Silver sword presented to Major Stewart by his fellow officers.
7. John Murray, 4th Duke of Atholl.
8. Landing of troops at Aboukir Bay.
9. Incident during George IV's visit to Edinburgh.
10. Statue of David Stewart.
11. David Stewart's burial place on St Lucia.

Acknowledgements

To Dr Joe Loudon, great-great-great nephew of David Stewart, and a constant source of help and encouragement, and to his third cousin, the late Alastair Irvine Robertson, who laid the foundations of this book.

With particular thanks to Alastair Steven, Jane Anderson, Charles Gore, Dr Jean Munro, John Prebble, Sylvia Robertson, Tom Smyth, Henry Steuart Fothringham, Roger Sylvester, and Muriel Walker.

James Irvine Robertson
Aberfeldy

Garth Castle, 1888, before restoration.

Foreword

THE TROPICAL DELUGE poured down. The steamy darkness was alive with ululating frogs and cicadas. Lanterns hanging on the peeling white columns of Government House lit a clutch of two-wheeled carriages, their canvas awnings swollen with water. The patient horses stood in harness with their ears flat against their heads and the warm rain dripping from their flanks. The coachmen were sipping rum in the slave quarters.

One animal pricked its ears at the sound of applause coming from an open window. In the reception room, lit by candelabra, a function was in progress and the Governor of St Lucia was about to make a speech. Slaves in white cotton – his Excellency could not afford to deck his staff in flunkeys' uniform – offered their master's own whisky to the planters and their wives. They wore shabby, old-fashioned silks and satins. Their language was French and Creole and the speaker's strong Scots accent would have them straining to understand.

The date was November 30th 1829, St Andrew's Night. The governor stood on a dais at the end of the room. He wore a kilt of Royal Stewart tartan, a tight green velvet jacket with silver buttons, diced stocking that scarcely covered his bulging calf muscles, and a white goatskin sporran. A dirk was thrust into his belt. He was a stocky little man in his late fifties, a bachelor, with a halo of white hair surrounding his bald head and a pair of silver-rimmed spectacles clamped to his nose. His right arm, crippled by old wounds, was carried awkwardly. In the candlelight his pate glistened with sweat.

'My heart is with you,' he began and this raised a huge cheer. A lump in his throat will have made him pause. He was an emotional man, always surprised and gratified by the high regard in which people held him. He went on to tell his guests that many people had tried to persuade him to stay at home and avoid the dangers of the West Indies. But now he was here, the friendship shown to him by St Lucians meant that he hardly missed Scotland – perhaps a gesture towards his garb raised an affectionate laugh at this point. In spite of the climate he said he would be happy to spend a hundred years amongst them.

The governor had been with them less than a year and he had already found a place in the hearts of almost all the islanders. Remarkably he did not enrich himself on commissions from granting slaves their freedom, nor did he take bribes.

And he certainly needed the money. His crushing debts were not his of own making but he had assumed responsibility for them since he felt that the honour of his family demanded it. He was a major-general, a hero of the Napoleonic Wars. He was a friend of royalty and yet his career had suffered for suspected Radicalism. He was beloved by the people of Scotland, particularly by his fellow Gaels, for he was a champion of the ordinary Highlander and a scathing critic of the clearance policies of his fellow lairds. And he had written one of the most influential books of the period which led his nation to redefine its own image.

But this was to be his last public appearance. In the words of his aide he was 'exerting himself very much'. He had recovered from an attack of fever in July and then removed himself to 'Pigeon island (a very healthy spot) where his health became perfectly re-established and he was looking better than I have ever seen him'. He returned to Government House to supervise preparations for his successful St Andrew's Night party. A few days afterwards, on 6th December, he was struck with illness, his symptoms 'fever, heaviness, and stupor'. It seems likely that a bout of benign malaria which was a regular feature of life in the tropics coincided with an attack of the malignant variety of the disease.

Tench, the government secretary, as well as two doctors remained constantly at Government House. So did the governor's aide, Blythe, who afterwards wrote this account of the subsequent days to the general's sister in Scotland. 'On the morning of the

12th he said to me "Blythe – I was just asking for you – I wish you to remain here as much as you can, but dont sit up at night for other people will do that" The Medical men there resorted to copious bleeding, mustard plasters were applied and a blister placed on the back of the neck but all these means would not drive away the intolerable heaviness and stupor that was upon him and in fact he hardly gave indications of feeling them.

'In the course of the day of the 16th a blister was applied to his head and on the morn of the 17th he had a most decided change for the better – so much so that I really began to have most sanguine hopes of his recovery but alas! – on the morning of the fatal day he again lapsed into his former heaviness, and fever increased when the medical Men told me that he could not properly recover.

'I went into the room when he said "Blythe I am afraid this is the end – this is the last" I replied "General, I have seen you worse so you must not despond." He then told me to get him a book from the library (the Peerage) and after that called for his spectacles. From then he began to sink very rapidly and at about ten minutes past 2 o'clock in the afternoon of the 18th breathed his last without a sigh, a struggle or a groan, indeed he just appeared as if falling asleep.

'His virtues and his talents endeared him to every body in the Island – they looked upon him not only as a Governor but as a Father and a friend – he had faithfully and fully discharged his duty to the Colony and of that they were very sensible. The people seem heartbroken about it and their conversation is "Alas! the poor general! We will never get such a man as General Stewart." I am mourning one from whom I have experienced not only the kindnesses and attentions of a Friend but those of a Father – he certainly was a second father to me'.

The news of the governor's death reached Scotland in February. Perhaps his obituary in the North Briton best summed up the man. 'He was the kindest, the gentlest, the best – without guile himself, and unsuspicious of it in other men – free from all manner of envy and uncharitableness – upright, generous, and friendly almost to a fault, and probably more generally esteemed and beloved than any other man of his time ... We despair of finding any one to fill the space occupied by him'.

CHAPTER ONE

Roots

'The centre of a social circle, where one is beloved and useful'

SOME PLACES SEEM like a blank canvas for each generation to mark as it chooses. Others have a framework which is immutable. The Vale of Fortingall in Highland Perthshire is one of the latter. Carved out by the glaciers, this fertile, flat-bottomed valley, five miles long and up to a mile wide, is really an extension of Glen Lyon but the entrance to that long winding corridor through the mountains is a narrow gorge which separates it from the last dash of its river across the vale to meet the Tay.

Two hundred years ago this landscape looked much the same as it does now. Then nearly a thousand souls[1] lived in this little glen amid its sheltering hills, now the figure is barely 150. Then the old clan battles and rivalries were within living memory; Gaelic was the spoken language and people could trace their ancestors back to those who 'first made smoke' in the district.

Now the old tongue is not heard and none of the descendants of the ancient proprietors or their tenants still live there. The village was rebuilt by a Victorian plutocrat; so was the church. South of the River Lyon rises the great forested whaleback of Drummond Hill, then owned by the mighty earls of Breadalbane who held land from this, the centre of Scotland, to the Atlantic. Like everyone else these Campbell potentates are long gone.

One family of lairds have left more of a mark than most. The venerable yew in the churchyard, reputed to be the oldest tree in Britain, has a sign that says it shades the burial plot of the Stewarts of Garth. Their estates began east of the market place on the rising land overlooking the standing stones and tumuli in the flat meadows by the river.

By the roadside at Keltneyburn where they had their mill,

smithy, and distillery stands a granite statue, larger than life, to the last of their number. In the 1950s, ceilidhs were held in its shadow. Jimmy Shand, the greatest Scottish dance band musician this century, would play there on summer evenings. Looking down from his high plinth, David Stewart would have approved for he was a friend of Niel Gow, Shand's most illustrious predecessor. The idealised stone figure – tall, straight and proud, with a noble profile – wears the uniform of a major of the Black Watch of 1801, his feather bonnet cradled in his right arm, his left hand resting on the hilt of his sword. The inscription reads:

> Major General
> David Stewart CB,
> of Drumcharry and Garth,
> Historian of the Highlands
> and the Highland Regiments,
> 1768–1829.
> Erected by
> The Stewart Society and other admirers
> in memory of
> A true Highlander.
> 1925.
> Cuimhnichibh na Doine o'n d'thainig sibh
>
> *(Remember the men from whom you have come)*

David Stewart would certainly have remembered the men from whom he had come, for lineage was central to the identity of Gaels like himself. His home had been a mile to the west. Set upon a mound amid young exotic trees, the simple two-storey house was stone under a slate roof. Above it to the north rose a craggy hill topped by the iron age fort of *Dun Geal*. From the window he could look out west, beyond the peat smoke rising from the little thatched cottages of the tenants, to the hills guarding Glen Lyon. Across the vale and the river French prisoners of war had toiled to lay drains for the Earl of Breadalbane on the flank of Drummond Hill where, in summer, fields of wheat grew 600 feet above the valley floor.

When David settled there in 1820 Drumcharry House had been the seat of his father, Robert Stewart, for more than half a century. He was known to the district as *Fear Ghart*, the Goodman of Garth. A widower for forty years, the laird was loved and respected throughout the district for his generosity and the concern he showed for the welfare of his tenantry.[2]

But in old age the laird was not the man he had been. In 1814 he had been affected by a stroke and he relied more and more on his heir William to run the estate. The eldest son had some training as a lawyer but he was a feeble man with a dull resentment of his younger brother's success. Running the house was the laird's spinster daughter, Clementina, about whom not a disparaging word has survived. Her younger sister Jessie was married with a growing family in the manse at Birnam across the Tay from Dunkeld, a brisk four hour's ride to the south. The youngest of the laird's three sons, John, was a planter in the West Indies.

The family traced their line back to the lawless and terrible Wolf of Badenoch, bastard of King Robert II. His son James settled at Garth Castle which controlled the hill pass, Glen Goulandie, between the straths of the rivers Tay and Tummel.

Walter Fitzalan, the original High Steward, arrived in Scotland as a henchman of King David in 1136. His origins were Breton. Other such immigrants were Norman. Some created their own clans – Menzies, whose chief had his seat a few miles downstream from Fortingall at Weem, Fraser, Hay, Lindsay, Murray, Grant, Graham and Cumming. The Bruces gave their country two monarchs, the Stewarts fourteen.

Fear Ghart was head of the Drumcharry line, an offshoot of the lairds of Duntanlich on Tummelside. In 1609 the family received a charter to their lands from Thomas Stewart of Grantully.[3] These stretched east from the market place at Fortingall opposite Drummond Hill and curved round the brae face that overlooked the Appin of Dull and Strathtay. The ploughable land amounted to little more than 300 acres.

Until the beginning of the eighteenth century, the lairds lived in the little, one-time Menzies castle of Comrie on the river Lyon just upstream from its confluence with the Tay. Then William Stewart chose the site at Drumcharry which was to remain the family seat for the next century. William's eldest son Patrick inherited the estate.

From the Duke of Atholl – a Murray whose forebear married the last Stewart heiress to the old earldom – the second son, Robert, obtained a tack, later converted to a charter, on the smaller estate of Garth whose lands adjoined Drumcharry and ran by the gorge of the Keltney burn up the pass of Glen Goulandie. The northern boundary was the ancient castle of Garth which had been rendered uninhabitable by Cromwell's soldiers.

In the next generation the second son of Drumcharry obtained a third estate of Inchgarth which lay to the north of the castle. Now three closely related Stewart lairds held land from Fortingall, round the corner above Coshieville, and north, almost to the watershed between straths Tay and Tummel. In the event of the failure of a male heir, each agreed to bequeath his estate to his kinsman's son in order to prevent the land leaving the family through the marriage of a daughter.

Down the centuries these lairds had married other Stewarts, Flemings, Menzieses, and Robertsons, thus knitting themselves into the kinship network of the eighty-odd landholding families that made up the ruling class in Atholl – once the Pictish kingdom of Fortran which covered most of Highland Perthshire – beneath the duke. Younger sons and daughters often married tenants on their fathers' estates and, by *Fear Ghart*'s time, many of the 600-odd folk on his lands could claim to be his kin and the descendants of kings.

Although of royal descent, albeit originally from the wrong side of the blanket, *Fear Ghart*'s forebears were an uncouth bunch. Patrick of Drumcharry was famous for his consumption of whisky. His grandfather in Cromwell's time preferred ale, then the usual tipple, and a song was written about his awesome capacity. Other members of the family were in trouble with the law for riot, for stealing a horse from the minister of Elie, for stabbing a Menzies.

The minister of Fortingall in 1699 describes William of Drumcharry, by then blind, and his family creating a disturbance in the kirk during service: 'His wife railed all ye tyme I was saying the blessing. They made such a noise & were in such a fury that I was necessitat to flie for it ... & Drumcharie's second son [Robert, later of Garth], who was cited to make penance yat day for fornication, lifted up his fist & cryed saying, "man, tho ye make your escape at this time I'lle make yow smart for it"'.[4]

A perennial problem for all three estates was the lack of shieling land where tenants could take their beasts in summer to graze. Rights on the hills were also needed for peat. The mountain pastures used by the tenants were disputed by the adjoining Campbells of Glenlyon whose lands met Drumcharry at Fortingall.

This unfortunate family had lost the major part of their holdings in Glen Lyon thanks to the dissipation and incompetence of Robert Campbell, commander of the company of the Argyll Regiment which perpetrated the Massacre of Glencoe in 1692. As Campbells they looked to the Earl of Breadalbane with his seat at the east end of Loch Tay, just over Drummond Hill from Fortingall, as their clan chief but the superiority of their properties lay with the Duke of Atholl. The tenants of the rival estates clashed periodically at the shielings and for the best part of a century their lairds clashed in the courts. The cost of these actions was a debilitating drain on the Stewart holdings.

At the time of the Rising of 1745, Drumcharry was possessed by the elderly, whisky-drinking Patrick Stewart whose son had no heir; Inchgarth was held by cousin Charles, Garth by another cousin, Black William. Drumcharry supported the government, Garth took his tenants to join Prince Charles and survived. Old Inchgarth's only son led his people in the charge of the Atholl Brigade at Culloden and was killed.[5] This left Black William's eldest son, Robert, heir to the three estates.

This Robert, *Fear Ghart*, inherited Garth in 1760 at the age of eighteen. His most influential guardian was his uncle, another Robert Stewart who was an Edinburgh lawyer known to his younger kinsmen and to most of the capital as Robbie Uncle. He arranged for his nephew to be apprenticed to a legal office in Dunkeld.[6] Since the '45 the Highlanders had been disarmed, their culture crushed, and now a laird's best weapon was an understanding of the law rather than the broadswords of his people.

Robbie Uncle also engineered a suitable spouse for his young nephew. Beyond Garth Castle, General Wade's military road – completed in 1733 to enable cannon to be carted into the mountains to subdue rebellious Highlanders – climbed over the pass of Glen Goulandie and descended into Strathtummel. There it ran through the lands of Kynachan and crossed the river by the three-arched Tummel Bridge which had been built for Wade by the proprietors of that estate. They, too, were Stewarts but from a different line from the nest of lairds over the pass.

Descendants of an illegitimate son of James II, they settled at Ballechin a dozen miles downstream of Fortingall near the confluence of the Tay and the Tummel. Unlike the Drumcharry family, they were cultivated people mixing with and marrying the aristocracy of Scotland. The lairds were chamberlains and bailies to the earls and marquesses of Atholl and were often their warlords. They were also fanatical Jacobites.

Patrick of Ballechin, Patrick of the Battles, took Blair Castle for Viscount Dundee and the deposed James VII in 1689 after William of Orange had been installed on the British throne.[7] The old warrior and his sons were reported to be the last to surrender when that rebellion collapsed after the Battle of Killiecrankie. One of these sons, John, acquired Kynachan.

In the Rising of 1715 he was a colonel in the Atholl Brigade and, captured at Preston, he lost his estate for three years.[8] His son David was major in the same battalion, Nairne's, in the '45. He was one of Lord George Murray's most trusted officers and considered responsible by the authorities for much of the Jacobite support in Atholl.[9] He and all save one of his tail of tenants died at Culloden. David's widow succeeded in holding on to his lands and two young girls were her heirs.

Unlike the three estates just across the pass, Kynachan had plenty of peat and shieling ground on Craig Kynachan as well as on the slopes of Schiehallion, the mountain whose name means the Seat of the Fairies of Caledonia. It would jigsaw neatly into young Robert of Garth's holdings and make him laird of land without break for eight miles between the rivers Lyon and Tummel.

The young man was betrothed to the eldest daughter of Kynachan, Janet, and married her in 1765 shortly after her mother's death. They lived in her mansion house until Robert inherited Drumcharry in 1776 a few years after the death of Uncle Inchgarth. The latter's will just needed to be settled and *Fear Ghart* would have possession of all four estates.

Although a strong supporter of the Union *Fear Ghart* lived like an old-fashioned Highland chief, the patriarch of his people and patron of their culture. He encouraged musicians and Gaelic bards, one of whom left a glowing panegyric – literally singing for his supper amid the candles and peatsmoke of the dining room at Drumcharry – to the laird's virtues. 'At balls the best dancer, Though skilled in knowledge and lear. The ardent moor-hunter, Whom hounds and glad gillies surround, In whose halls wine, venison, salmon, For comers abound. Hospitality's prince, To guests and relatives kind, Good chieftain of tenants, Who frowns not when rent is behind.'[10]

David later described the richness of the rewards to such benevolent autocrats as his father. 'To those who live in the busy world, and are hurried round by its agitations, it is difficult to form an idea of the means by which time may be filled up and interest excited in families who, through choice or necessity, dwell among their own people.

'The secret lies in the excitement of strong attachment. To be in the centre of a social circle where one is beloved and useful, to be able to mould the characters and direct the passion by which one is surrounded, creates, in those whom the world has not hardened, a powerful interest in the most minute circumstances which gives pleasure or pain to any individual in that circle where so much affection and good will are concentrated. The mind is stimulated by stronger excitements and a greater variety of enjoyments than matters of even the highest importance can produce in those who are rendered callous by living amongst the selfish and the frivolous. It is not the importance of the objects but the value at which they are estimated that renders their moral interest permanent and salutary.'[11]

But *Fear Ghart* had another side to his nature. David is again the informant. 'My father was fierce and violent in his temper – his passions often overturned his reason, and he broke loose in his language ... if he was called a kind master to tenants and saw his table full, and he was called hospitable, he looked not to the consequences for his family.'[12] The old lawyer, Robbie Uncle, had occasion to rebuke his nephew in 1766 when he broke the law by selling an impecunious tenant's livestock. In another questionable example of *Fear Ghart*'s practice, he was sued by other tenants when he broke their lease by stripping their land of all crops just before they moved in. He was also less than generous when his sister-in-law eloped with the landless son of a tenant in 1768. As well as a magistrate and a commissary at the church court at Dunkeld for a time he was a factor to the 4th Duke of Atholl but he was sacked.

'I don't intend to say but that you mean well', wrote His Grace in 1795, 'but I mean to say you have not got that capacity for energy and exertion which is requisite in a person who has the charge of an estate such as mine. I do not want to part with you in anger; on the contrary, I am ready to do anything which can be reasonably asked for yourself and family.'[13]

However the dismissal may have resulted from disagreements over policy as much as incompetence. The duke who would live until 1830 complained that 'In Dividing of Farms, in letting of Farms, in maintaining among the Tennantry a satisfaction in these farms, in making stated and regular accounts, I have received no satisfaction from you'. *Fear Ghart* was famous as friend to the country people; he would be most unwilling to take measures that would oust any of the existing tenants.

When Uncle Inchgarth died in 1765 he had indeed bequeathed his estate to Robert as the agreement between the cousins had stipulated but his will left the rents to his own daughter Ann for her lifetime. *Fear Ghart* went to law and produced a dubious document which said that the old man had changed his mind but Ann had financial support from the Campbells of Glenlyon who saw a chance to damage their rivals.

With his cousin enjoying the fruits of the estate, *Fear Ghart* chased the case through the courts, losing his final appeal in the House of Lords in 1784, and Ann lived on another dozen years before he gained possession. The consequence of these actions was debts that would later jeopardise the family's hold on the estates.

CHAPTER TWO

To be a Soldier

'*A strong propensity for the Military Line*'

DAVID, OUR PROTAGONIST, was the third child of the marriage, probably being born at Kynachan in 1772. As was customary, he was named after his maternal grandfather, his elder brother being baptised William after his father's father. Only one of the family has his baptism in the parish register, the likely reason being that their mother inherited the Episcopalian persuasion of her parents, and the records of this church, suppressed after the '45, have disappeared.

After the family moved to Drumcharry the boys still spent their spare time and their summers in Strathtummel. William was sickly but studious. David was small, fair, short-sighted, tough, vigorous, and spirited. He was said to have always been scampering about the countryside, mixing freely and easily with the children of the tenants. Bilingual, he spoke the Gaelic language of the people as fluently as he could speak, and write, the English language by then used by the lairds.

The mansion house at Kynachan, another modest two-storey building, had survived the depredations of the Argyll Militia after Culloden. They had looted the estate – an estate of widows since the battle, as the duke's bailie observed in his journal – but the house had been spared the torch since its proximity to Tummel Bridge made it potentially useful as a barracks.

Now Duncan McDiarmid rented the house and farmed the in-by land. He was the son of a notable local character, Baron McDiarmid, whose family's roots in the area went back to time immemorial. From him David heard all the ancient stories and legends of Atholl and Gaeldom. At the feet of Duncan's niece and housekeeper Catherine Macarthur, the boy absorbed the songs and the music.

At Pitkerril, one of the Kynachan farms high up in the shadow of Schiehallion, lived David's aunt Euphemia and her family. She was his mother's younger sister and had created a great commotion before David was born by slipping from the mansion house in the middle of the night, leaving a letter on her table. This announced that she was eloping with Mungo Reid, the landless son of a Culloden widow who lived on the nearest of the estate's townships. The local people hugely enjoyed the scandal and soon a song was doing the rounds: 'Good luck to Mungo Reid who stole the heiress of Kynachan'.[14] After a few miserable years in Edinburgh the couple returned to the estate as tenants where they lived into old age, both dying in 1825.

David's mother Janet was a thoroughly decent woman – she died when he was 13 – but Euphemia was more clever and, as her history might suggest, more romantic in nature. The two sisters had been babies during the Rising. Their home had been occupied by the soldiers of the Argyll Militia who were captured when Lord George Murray marched the Atholl Brigade south a month before Culloden and, in darkness, took more than 30 enemy outposts before besieging his brother's castle at Blair.

Following the final battle and the collapse of the Rising the laird of Kynachan's widow, the eldest child of an Edinburgh lawyer, had gone to the courts to protect herself and her tenants from further looting by government troops and had used considerable subtlety to ensure that she and her family continued to hold the estate. In spite of the strong disapproval of the authorities she, alone along the Tummel, had remained an Episcopalian – the denomination of the Jacobite lairds.

From Euphemia David learned of the central role played by his ancestors in a century of civil wars in support of the Stuart kings. The pink glow of romance had already coloured the horrors of this period and his aunt's stories would have had the smooth patina of 30 years of telling.

The boy grew up steeped in the Gaelic culture. He earned the respect and affection of the country people and this was reciprocated. They would have wanted to think well of him because the

Gaels honoured their chiefs and lairds. For generations their own ancestors had fought in the tails of David's forebears who were the boughs of the genealogical trees of which the ordinary Highlanders were so proud to be twigs. By the 1770s most of the aristocracy of Gaeldom had decided that their future lay in the mainstream of Scottish and United Kingdom culture. *Fear Ghart* preferred the old ways and taught them to his children.

Robert Stewart's sons went to the parish school in Fortingall under the dominie Neil McIntyre. He was an excellent teacher but unpopular with the minister since he gave more time to study of the classics than to the Bible.[15] David shared a bench with the sons of tenants as well as with an embryo knight and a future Fortingall minister who would become his own brother-in-law. Another pupil, a few years older, would command the Black Watch.

William was destined to be laird but the younger sons would have to make their own way in life. David could have chosen the law, the church, or trade which in Scotland was considered a perfectly respectable occupation for a gentleman – as was the profession of 'manufacturer' which was once planned for John, David's rather stolid younger brother. Equally popular was sugar planting in the West Indies which had been the career of one of *Fear Ghart*'s siblings. But David chose to be a soldier.

In 1739 the 42nd (Royal Highland – The Black Watch) Regiment had been the first body of Highlanders incorporated into the British Army. After the hiccup of a mutiny in 1743 the regiment had shown itself to be a formidably efficient body of fighting men. It had also given a very useful military education to many of the rebel officers, such as Charles Stewart of Bohally – married to David's great aunt – and another source of spellbinding tales for the boy.

It had been the elder Pitt who realised he could solve several problems at once by taking up the Duke of Cumberland's suggestion of adding to the army's Highland Regiments. Such formations would soak up the warriors of the glens who had been such a source of trouble in the past. The Highlanders could provide the government with politically unimportant arrow and spear fodder in colonial wars in India and America.

The chiefs had packed as many fighting men as they could onto their estates but now they were interested in cash rents to support a gentleman's lifestyle in Edinburgh or London. The recruitment into the army of the surplus of young men took some of the pressure off the land and brought in money when they sent their pay home and capital when they returned with loot and prize money.

Quite apart from providing colonels, majors, and captains for rebel armies, David's family already had more conventional military connections. Behind the mansion house of Drumcharry *Fear Ghart* supported a school which trained young men to become pipers in the army. The kilt, tartan, the broadsword and all weapons had been banned after the Rising – except in the service of His Majesty. This had been a stroke of genius by the government. In the Highland regiments and only in the Highland regiments could the young Gael enjoy, like his forefathers, the warrior culture and all its trappings.

Fear Ghart's uncle Neil had joined Montgomerie's Highlanders. His brother William had been a captain in the 42nd Regiment before entering the Dutch service. Another brother, Charles, along with the sons of other local lairds, was in the 77th Foot, the Athole Highlanders, the regiment raised by the Duke in 1777. Lieutenant Stewart came home to Drumcharry on sick leave in 1781 when, although the regiment had been peacefully stationed in Ireland, he no doubt inspired his nephew with martial tales.

On 27th April 1781, *Fear Ghart* wrote to Col James Murray, uncle to the young duke and son of Prince Charles' general Lord George Murray, who was in command of the 77th, inquiring about the possibility of David being recommended for an ensigncy in his regiment. 'I have a young boy that discovers a strong propensity for the Military Line. I would wish to yield to his inclination ... The boy is young, not yet full fourteen, and low stature, but well made and strong. I may probably be thought a partiall Judge, but others agree that he is very promising, so that want of years is a fault that is always mending. My brother would supply any defect of duty, till he shall be able himself. The boy's name is David'.[16]

His father was stretching the point somewhat. Eleven was quite a usual age to obtain a commission; thirteen and a half, the age at which Lord William Murray was appointed ensign in the 42nd Regiment in 1775, was getting on a bit. David had enjoyed his birthday on 12th April[17] but he could not have been thirteen which would have had him born in 1768. At least two children died between the birth of William in 1766 and David, and the boy was most likely nine when his father first applied to Colonel Murray.

One can presume he replied that a lad so young and so short was of little use to the army until either of these conditions had been rectified. So *Fear Ghart* tried again. This time a week before his son's eleventh birthday.

The men of the Athole Highlanders had originally enlisted for three years or the duration of the war against America. When peace was declared in January 1783 the regiment, already shipped from Ireland to southern England, was ordered to march to Portsmouth where they expected to be discharged. Instead they were told that they were bound for the East Indies. The notion grew that they had been betrayed by their officers and were to be sold to the East India Company. They refused to board the transports and rioted.

They broke into the military stores and got drunk. One invalid soldier on guard duty was killed by their *feu de boire* and the officers only just escaped with their lives. The following morning the men had sobered up and paraded as normal. Lord George Lennox came down from the capital to tick them off and assure them they would not be sent abroad. Before the general had time to return to his duties as MP and constable of the Tower of London he was called on again, this time to roast the men of the 68th who rioted four days later for precisely the same reason as the 77th.[18]

No punishments were inflicted on the Highlanders and they were ordered back to Scotland. In February whilst on the march the news came through that they were to be disbanded the following month.

Officers' commissions were a regimental colonel's to sell. Murray would ensure he had realised all his assets before the 77th was broken up. On the 3rd April, *Fear Ghart* wrote to the now Major-General Murray.[19] He replied that an ensigncy was available. Although he had received several applications for this commission he favoured David, had appointed him, and *Fear Ghart* now owed 200 guineas. Little more than a week after David was gazetted the regiment was broken up and the new ensign placed on half pay to continue his education at home.

The Duke was the feudal superior of the estates of Drumcharry, Garth and Kynachan and for centuries the ducal family had been the source of patronage in Atholl. So it was natural that *Fear Ghart* would turn to the Athole Regiment when he sought David's commission. However, he was still being a little premature. It may be that he was seizing his moment, afraid he would no longer have influence with a regimental commander when David was a year or two older or it may have been that his son's half-pay gave a reasonable return on the capital invested so long as he remained at Drumcharry.

In August 1787, aged 15 and now acquainted with French, Spanish and German, David joined the Black Watch. Two new companies were raised which joined the regiment on its return from Canada where it had been stationed following the War of American Independence. The Highlanders marched to Scotland where they would be located for the next six years. The new officer was given a wise old soldier William Fraser, as his servant and this man, who called his master *Daibhidh Ban* – fair-haired Davie – rather than 'sir', taught the young ensign his trade as a commander of Gaelic-speaking soldiers.

Whilst based at Stirling Castle in the summer of 1792 the regiment was reviewed by General Leslie, and on 17th July David and 17 of his fellow officers received a modest piece of parchment granting them the Freedom of the Royal Burgh. But this was the 'Year of the Sheep', the ominous precursor of the Sutherland Clearances. Certain gentlemen of Ross-shire had decided to replace their tenants with lowland graziers who would pay a higher rent. Most of the native inhabitants were ejected from their farms. After some months the remaining people cleared the hills of the interloping beasts and drove them beyond the county boundary without so much as stealing a single lamb chop.

'To quell these tumults', wrote David thirty years later 'occasioned little less alarm among some of the gentlemen of Ross than the Rebellion of 1745. The 42nd Regiment was ordered to proceed, by forced marches and by the shortest routes, to Ross-shire. When they reached the expected scene of action, there was, fortunately, no enemy; for the people had separated and disappeared of their own accord'.[20] Eighteen men were arrested as ringleaders, tried, found guilty, and sentenced to be transported to Botany Bay. The appeal system was more crude then than now, but highly effective. 'The men disappeared out from prison, no one knew how, and were never inquired after or molested'.

The regiment was quickly ordered back to the Lowlands where the people were just as restive and less reticent in expressing it but the Ross-shire incident made a deep impression on young Ensign Stewart. He described the removals as 'cold-hearted' and wrote that 'the manner in which the people gave vent to their grief and rage when driven from their ancient homes showed that they did not merit this treatment'. However, what impressed him most was the discipline of his own soldiers. Although they had every sympathy with the plight of their fellow-Highlanders, some of whom had friends and relations in the regiment, they never wavered in the execution of their duty.

The Black Watch was ordered abroad in 1793. Stewart, returning from four months leave at home, was now twenty-one, five foot six inches tall and short-sighted, but he had a strong constitution, limitless courage, limitless self-confidence, and limitless ambition. Since his promotion would depend upon merit rather than purchase he would always be assiduous in ensuring that his qualities caught the attention of his superiors. Over the next 20 years the battles against Revolutionary France would bring him fame throughout Scotland and admiration from the tens of thousands of his peers who fought in the war.

CHAPTER THREE

Campaigns in the West Indies

*'The cruelties the Enemy have exercised wherever they
had the opportunity in this country is beyond anything I
ever heard'*

THE NATURE of the men David Stewart would command changed during his career. Initially the Highland soldiers were all volunteers but the demand for manpower to serve in the army and navy during the decades of the wars against France would lead to conscription.

The society from which these men were recruited would also change and after retiring from active service Stewart would devote much of his great work, "Sketches of the Character, Manners, and Present State of the Highlanders of Scotland with details of the Military Service of the Highland Regiments" to explaining the change and its causes.

Two new companies of Highlanders were added to the 42nd in time for the embarkation for Flanders, and 'on the whole, these were good men, but not the same description with those who, in former times, were so ready to join the standard of the Black Watch'.[21] The older men had been the children of the old patriarchal warrior culture that had its origins before the '45. They considered the army to be the most honourable of professions, and their officers took the place of the chieftains who had formed such a close fighting relationship with their tails. Very different were the men of the English regiments of the line. For them the army was often the only alternative to jail.

The new recruits joined the 42nd at Montrose and the regiment marched to Musselburgh in May 1793 where they embarked for Hull. For more than a year they moved to and fro across the North Sea and the Channel to counter movements of the French, without seeing action. Finally, in June 1794, the Highlanders joined the army at Ostend.

In the campaigns in the Low Countries, troops came from Britain, Holland, Austria, Prussia, Spain, and Sardinia. The contemporary view of the affair was not flattering to the British commander. Lieutenant Stewart was one of those under the grand old Duke of York and the young officer did his fair share of marching up and down as one of the ten thousand over the next eight months of futile activity.

The winter was the worst in memory. Brandy froze in the flask and the Dutch barred their doors against the soldiers whether wounded or merely frostbitten. As Stewart later recorded, their misery 'has only been exceeded by the sufferings of the French in their disastrous retreat from Moscow'.[22] Disease amongst the troops was widespread and David proudly recorded that the 42nd lost only twenty five men whilst some of the other regiments lost more than 300 through sickness or through becoming exhausted by the arctic conditions and falling into enemy hands.

The 42nd returned to England in April 1794 to camp near Chelmsford where they were joined by drafts from various regiments being broken up. To Stewart's chagrin the Black Watch ended up with five captains too many, and each of these would have to be found a company before promotion could be expected for more junior officers.

In October, the regiment arrived at Portsmouth to join Sir Ralph Abercromby's expeditionary force – the largest that had ever sailed from Britain – to the West Indies where they would fight the French for control of the islands and the sugar trade.

David kept a rough journal on the voyage, and wrote of it further in the Sketches. The force consisted of more than 22,000 soldiers and 3,000 cavalry horses which required more than 300 ships to convey them across the Atlantic. The commander decided to sail in one vast fleet from Portsmouth but the time of year was unpropitious. David with 500 men of the Black Watch was on board the *Middlesex*. During his first night watch on 26th October 'at 12 past 12 came on a most tremendous gale which continued till seven in the morning'.

The admiral's ship ran aground and the fleet's departure was delayed until 15th November. The East Indiaman carrying the five companies of the 42nd lost its bowsprit in collision with a frigate and was still being repaired in harbour when, on 20th November, most of the fleet limped back to port having encountered another storm. Several ships and many lives had been lost. On 9th December they were off again, met yet another gale which scattered the fleet and David reported he was 'much distressed with sea sickness'. By 22nd December the Middlesex was by itself.

They spotted Madeira at 7 am on the 9th of January. At 8 am, 'sighting two strange sail – cleared for action – but running away all the time as fast as we could', they lost their pursuers at dusk. The *Middlesex* met other vessels of the fleet but never managed to keep them in sight overnight. On the 24th they met the trade winds and David remarks, 'Moderate and pleasant weather, the first comfortable day since I left England'.

On 5th February the ship dropped anchor in Carlisle Bay, Barbados and found only six of the fleet already there. For a month they swung at their mooring, not allowed ashore, while the rest of the ships straggled into the harbour. Half the regiment never made it. Their ship had been forced back to Portsmouth and these men were eventually sent to Gibraltar.

80,000 men of the British army died in the West Indies during the years 1793–6. By far the greatest danger was fever, which killed twenty times as many troops as the enemy. The Highlanders discarded their plaids, kilts, and feather bonnets and instead wore round felt hats and linen pantaloons. On the evening of 21st March the *Middlesex* sailed for Martinique. At the harbour mouth the ship's rigging became entangled with the *Minotaur* of 74 guns which became stuck on a sandbank. Whilst this was being sorted out, the five companies of Highlanders were allowed ashore for the first time in five months.

Under Brigadier-General (later Sir John) Moore a brigade was ordered to St Lucia. Provisions for two days were cooked and the troops re-embarked for the 24 mile crossing to the French-occupied island. The 42nd made the first landing unopposed on 26th April. David's journal is hastily jotted notes. On the voyage it details latitude and longitude each day, ships sighted, and the weather. Once ashore on St Lucia it lasts but four days into the month-long campaign before falling silent.

Thirteen British regiments have St Lucia amongst their battle honours. The island had been fought over by the British and French since the mid-seventeenth century and, during the Revolutionary and Napoleonic Wars, it changed hands six times. It was a hellish place for a soldier. Infested by poisonous snakes, hot, humid, swampy jungle clothed rocky ridges and gullies. Four out of five of the general's command would be buried on the island, the vast majority succumbing to yellow fever, malaria, or a host of other diseases. The 31st Regiment was 915 strong when it landed in May 1796. When it left in December, just 74 men were still alive.[23]

Landings were made both north and south of the fortress of Morne Fortune which dominated the harbour and the war-ravaged capital of Castries. With great difficulty guns were dragged across the ravines and the ridges to positions where they could bombard the French defences. David spent 17 days in charge of 60 men at an outpost commanding a pass close to the enemy. He was never relieved because, in the words of Sir Ralph Abercromby, 'an intelligent Officer in whom he placed confidence was requir'd for that Post'.[24] On one occasion the French threatened an attack and the general was advised to send reinforcements. 'It is not necessary,' he said. 'Captain D. Stewart and a part of the 42nd occupies the Post and will defend themselves'.

On 16th May, David found time to write a short note to his father. 'With some difficulty I have procured this piece of paper to say that after being exposed to the dews of the nights and the heat of Mid-day in St. Lucia, where, I have often been told at home, that if a man lay one night on the ground, he would certainly lose the power of the side he lay upon before morning,

I am in perfect good health and spirits as much as ever ... Sandy and James Clochfoldich are both well. Tell Mr Robertson McGrigor, with my compts. that his son Bob is very well, and that I had the pleasure of seeing him in a smart but short action we had lately, behave himself in manner worthy of the name, and a descendant of clan McGrigor. In eight days at most this island will be in our possession'.[25]

Many of the officers and men of the Black Watch were from Highland Perthshire. Sandy and James were both sons of the laird of Clochfoldich, a longtime Stewart estate an hour and a half's ride down the Tay from Drumcharry. Mr McGrigor was probably even more local. Just as *Fear Ghart* would have told his neighbours about his son's letter and the mention of young Bob's gallantry, so other soldiers would have written home about David Stewart. Thus his fame and reputation would grow throughout his own country, more effectively than if, like his elder brother, he had remained at home.

David was correct in his forecast of a French surrender within eight days. From St Lucia the regiment was shipped 40-odd miles south to invade St Vincent. David again distinguished himself.

The British, directly under Abercromby, landed on June 8 and found the French occupying a chain of four redoubts which they considered impregnable. After two days of preparation the Highlanders were sent forward to make a feint attack on the first position, situated on a ridge above a steep slope, to test its strength. The feint turned real and within half an hour the enemy had been driven from the first three redoubts.

Stewart pushed forward with some 30 men of the 42nd to the base of the last stronghold where, sheltered from the guns above, they waited for reinforcements before storming the final defences. Meantime the captured French commander had realised the position of this last garrison was hopeless and agreed to order its defenders to march out after sunset and surrender.

From the third redoubt the colonel signalled to David to withdraw. In the dash across the open ground the enemy opened fired, killing six of the Highlanders and wounding seven. The French broke the truce that night and several hundred escaped to the woods from where they fought a 16-week guerrilla campaign.

After a month on the island David wrote a long letter home. He describes the bitter nature of the fighting. The capture of one of the enemy posts 'did not last above half an hour, we had thirty seven men killed and wounded, and one officer wounded slightly – had we gone on to the fourth post we should have lost many more, for such is the inveteracy of our men against the enemy that they would give no quarter, and I am unfeeling enough to say (but I believe that on these occasions feelings are entirely out of the question) that I would not restrain them. The cruelties the Enemy have exercised wherever they had the opportunity in this country is beyond anything I ever heard'.[26]

He goes on to say that half of the Regiment was now unfit for duty but he had never felt better in his life and was one of only two officers so blessed. A local planter returning home to Montrose was the bearer of the letter. He had lent David a horse and the grateful officer asks that his father send a flock of assorted fowl – guinea fowl and 'the large black white-headed barn fowls Clemy got from Dunkeld' – to his benefactor as recompense.

Although the general on St Lucia had referred to him as a captain, he was still a lieutenant. Major Christie who had joined the regiment with Ensign Stewart nine years earlier had just died of fever. David describes how he went to General Abercromby to point out that he was now the oldest lieutenant in the regiment and had served 13 years in the army. *Fear Ghart* had shot his financial bolt with his purchase of the ensigncy and his son thenceforward had to rely on his pay and prize money.

Abercromby said that his claim was good and, had Christie died in battle, a promotion could have been handed out on the spot but he died of fever and official channels must be followed. 'I could not help thinking this a nice distinction, whether a man died in consequence of the necessary and unavoidable fatigues of his duty, or by the shot of the enemy. However I said nothing, but thanked him, made my bow, and walked off – But I won't give up the point yet. I'll have another trial, and secure the interest of the General's son and his Secretary, both of whom I know will speak in my favour. At all events I hope he will be prevailed upon to appoint me to do duty as captain till His Majesty's pleasure is known. This will secure us rank and pay from the day Major Christie died'.

David then talks about the cost of living: 'a fellow won't blush to ask me six dollars for a Turkey, half a crown for a lb of mutton, and what is still more remarkable three shillings for a lb of lump sugar – the natural product of the country'.

Before concluding he writes: 'I am rather at a loss for the want of my servant, who was shot through both thighs on the tenth ... I had eleven men of the company I command killed and wounded the same day, indeed it was all in a few minutes. I am sorry to tell Clemy that the Parrots I bought for her are dead. When we first took the field I gave them in charge of an old black rascal who allowed them to die for want of proper attention'.

The ensuing fighting was bloody. David, of course, took a prominent part.

CHAPTER FOUR

Jungle Warfare

'In forty years I might be worth near sixteen hundred pounds'

DURING THE CAMPAIGN Stewart was frequently skirmishing with the enemy, many of whom were slaves freed by the revolutionary French, or local militia and other irregulars whom the British described as 'brigands'. In the *Sketches* he writes vividly of one of these encounters. The army was harassed by snipers firing at sentries during the night and David resolved to seek out their camp.

'I obtained leave from the general to select a party, consisting of a sergeant and twelve men, and entered the woods at nine o'clock at night, guiding myself by the compass, and the natural formation of the country, which consisted of parallel ridges divided by deep ravines formed by the mountain torrents. The men were provided with strong short cutlasses to cut their way through the underwood, without which it would have been impossible to penetrate unless we should accidentally have fallen in with a foot-path frequented by the Caribbs.

'In this slow progress, nothing occurred till soon after sun-rise when traces were discovered of people having lately passed through the woods; the undergrowth being thinner, the men could move on with less noise in clearing an opening. More evident indications appearing that this place had been frequented, I directed the sergeant to follow me, leaving the men to rest, and crept to a little distance in the hope of finding some opening in the woods.

'We had not gone five hundred paces when on a sudden we came to an open spot on which stood a man with a musquet, apparently as a sentinel. The instant he saw us he presented his piece, when a small spaniel which followed me sprang forward and seized him by the foot. In the agitation of alarm or pain, the man discharged his musket at the dog, and, plunging into the woods, was out of sight in an instant before the sergeant who attempted to cut him down with his sword could get near him.

'We were now on an elevated spot with a few feet of clear ground, and on the edge of a perpendicular precipice of great depth, at the bottom of which was seen a small valley with a crowd of huts, from which swarms of people sprung out when they heard the report of the musket.

'Satisfied that this was the place we were in search of, I immediately retraced my steps; but we had not marched half way when we were attacked on both flanks and rear by the enemy, who followed the party. Being excellent climbers, they seemed in an instant to have manned the trees. The wood was in a blaze, but not a man was to be seen, all being perfectly covered by the luxuriant foliage. I directed the men to keep themselves as much as possible under cover, and to retreat from tree to tree firing at the spot where they perceived the fire of the enemy who followed with as much rapidity as if they had sprung like monkeys from tree to tree'.[27]

The general sent out a rescue party when the firing was heard but six men were killed and eight wounded. The fate of the gallant spaniel was not recorded.

After months of this sort of fighting, David received a letter from *Fear Ghart*. He reported fine crops at home, a source of enormous relief when poor harvests could still lead to starvation. He must also have aired his concern about the future of his youngest son John for David replies on the subject at some length and displays a maturity and confidence in his opinions – and a hint of pomposity – which is unexpected from a 24 year-old to his 60 year-old father. His sickly elder brother William was already fading into inconsequentiality and it seems that David, in spite of his absence in the King's service, was the son whose opinion *Fear Ghart* respected.

'I can easily believe that you are much perplexed about John;' wrote David. 'It is a delicate and difficult thing to make a proper choice. To every profession of which I can think so many objections appear that I am sure I know not what to advise. Owing to the deficiency in his education which I have long with pain observed, and have so often advised him on the subject, and pointed out to him the ill effects, and unavoidable poor future he would make in the world in consequence of his negligence that I believe he was heartily glad when I was separated from him.

'The army in that respect is the properest profession for him as experience is the best criterion to form a judgement. I hope I shall be allowed to say that in every other respect that of arms is the least eligible profession for a young man in his situation without much money or interest.

'Perhaps it may be said that the want of the former in particular is applicable to all professions, allowing it to be so in the first outset, still in all other professions by a care, diligence and attention a man has the power of realising some little stock. But in mine if I am economical enough to live on half my annual income and lay up the other, perhaps in forty years I might be worth near sixteen hundred pounds.

'If he is fully determined to be a manufacturer, Glasgow is much to be preferred to Perth or any other town in Scotland, as it is there only that he can gain a proper knowledge of that line of business. But there are very capital objections – the dissolute manners of the young men and the expense of living, which is nearly a third more than Perth. For the latter I fear there is no remedy and with pleasure I believe that there is less risk of his being ruined by the former than most young men. I have always found him very prudent and guarded in his conduct, and in general averse to follow his companions in any of their wild frolics.

'But in case that the manufacturing plan shall be given up, I certainly recommend a trial of his fortune in this island. There is not in His Majesty's dominions a place where a young man with common abilities, diligence, and perserverence will more quickly realise an independency than in this small colony. I don't speak of its present date which is one continued scene of waste and desolation. But that which a few months of peace and tranquillity will bring about.

'The climate to be sure is bad but I am convinced from my own experience and what I have observed in others, that by a prudent regular manner of living, the greater part of its bad effects may be avoided. This holds particularly true with regard to St Vincent which is remarkably healthy.

'Among many instances, independent of the healthy jolly appearance of the people, I will only give you one – that the 35th Regt were quartered here some years, and only lost by sickness thirteen men in all that time, though the Regt was near 500 strong. However you'll observe that they had plenty of good provisions, good accommodation and nothing to do – our situation being very different we suffer accordingly'.[28]

It should be remembered that David was in the midst of a vicious little jungle war. When he was not fighting and caring for his own men, he was acting as 'Commanding Officer, Adjutant Quarter-Master, and Paymaster; as all the Officers except two and myself were totally disabled by sickness and debility'. He was actually in command of all five companies of the Black Watch. Any spare time one would think he would spend in relaxation. And yet he seems to have been making an appraisal of the potential of St Vincent.

'The fertility of this Island is certainly wonderful, a planter will consider his crop very deficient if it does not produce him a nett clearance of twenty pounds sterling the acre!! I write this near Alexr Macdougall's estate which is not quite 300 acres including the ground on which his own house stood, and his Negro houses and gardens. The crop that was on the ground when the whole was burnt and laid waste by the enemy would have produced £9,000 sterling!! [Multiply by fifty for rough modern equivalents] but such is the enormous expense of labouring the land that £5,000 would have been appropriated to that purpose.

'I dare say you will hardly give credit to this though I can assure you nothing is more true. I could give you many more instances, but one is sufficient. They sow small quantities of a kind of Indian corn on their detached pieces of ground, forty and fifty bolls of our measure the acre is the common produce. I can arm you with a number of particulars when I return home.

'From the very state I have been in these last months I have not the power of procuring the necessary information about settling John in this Island. It is the only one in the West Indies I would recommend should you resolve to send him out. I therefore cannot pretend to give a proper determined opinion on the subject. However I hope by the time that the next packet sails our troubles will be over and I will be able to give you the requisite information, and that with the beginning of a few hundred pounds John will have a fair chance of making a fortune, that is if you and he are willing to try the experiment.

'If he is not perfectly willing himself I would never press him. If a man is forced or even overadvised to any particular line of business, the chance of succeeding in that line is little and lays a foundation for after reprehension and unavailing reflection on the advisers'.

After the capture of St Vincent, Trinidad soon surrendered to Sir Ralph Abercromby and he moved on to Porto Rico. This island's Gibraltar-like fortress proved too tough a nut and the British made a fighting withdrawal. By this stage of the campaign David Stewart had become one of the general's most trusted officers and was being used by him for the most important duties. On this occasion the new captain was stationed on a bridge which controlled the only possible route whereby the French could attack the expeditionary force as it re-embarked.

The Regiment then returned to the UK, landing in Portsmouth on 30th July 1797. David's promotion to Captain Lieutenant was waiting for him, backdated to 24th June 1796, a fortnight after he had petitioned the general in Barbados. He was now 25 and a highly effective commander of Highland troops but there was no time to visit home for within a few weeks the Regiment was shipped to the Mediterranean.

Whilst it was on the high seas, dramatic events were taking place back home in Atholl. A Militia Act, the results of which would later impinge on David's career, had been passed which allowed for a balloted conscription to provide men to defend the country in the event of a French invasion. The people feared a ruse to ship their young men to the West Indies where they would inevitably die of fever.

In Highland Perthshire there were riots. For some days crowds of up to 15,000 people washed up and down the straths, ignoring authority and forcing lairds to sign documents of support. William Stewart, younger of Garth, made his small mark on history when he took charge of the Fortingall Parish Register which was the source of names of those to be balloted. He was confronted by the rioters, an old lady threw a blanket over his head, and the Register was thrown into a ditch. The resulting water damage is the despair of modern genealogists.

William was then carried by the mob a couple of miles east to Castle Menzies where an enormous crowd forced Sir John Menzies to sign their paper. To the north the Duke of Atholl called out his tenants and some 400 of them paraded with cudgels, scythes, and dung forks to defend Blair Castle should the rabble attack.

Ten days later the episode collapsed into near farce when a small detachment of soldiers trotted into Strathtay, arrested James Cameron, the reluctant leader of the rioters, and bundled him into a coach. In the dawn light they carried him through mobs of several thousand people without interference and eventually lodged him in jail in Edinburgh. Astonishingly Cameron was released on bail and he promptly disappeared.[29]

John Stewart had missed all this excitement for he had followed his brother's advice and left Highland Perthshire to become part-owner of the Parkhill Plantation in St Vincent. His sleeping partner, owning both slaves and a share of the property, was David himself.

It may seem incongruous that a man who was later to become such a champion of the rights of the ordinary Highlander should own slaves but the sugar plantations of the Americas were established parts of the economies of Holland, France, Spain, and the United States, as well as Britain. The United Kingdom had banned the slave trade but it was to be another generation before slavery itself would be abolished in the British colonies, a process in which David himself would play a small part. Meantime he could count scores of friends and acquaintances who still worked the plantations or whose families had made fortunes in the West Indies over the previous 150 years.

When David was there the islands were at war, their economies had ceased to function, and the Negroes were being slaughtered, starved, or caught up in the fighting. It was then that he became owner of a few slaves, probably through no more than paying for their food, shelter, and accepting responsibility for them. They were waiting for brother John when he went out and provided the nucleus of his labour force.

The army in the Mediterranean of which David was a part took Minorca without a shot being fired. Little more was achieved. A raid on Cadiz was mounted and the troops designated for the assault had already transferred from the transports to the boats for the run to shore when a flag of truce came out from the city. Pestilence was raging and thousands had already died. The attack was aborted and the fleet returned to Gibraltar. At some time during this period, Stewart's ship was taken by the Spaniards and he was made prisoner for five months. He busied himself by improving his Spanish before an exchange was arranged and, after a short leave in Scotland, he rejoined his Regiment on Minorca. The next operation would bring him glory.

CHAPTER FIVE

A Hero of Alexandria

'God bless you, Captain Stewart; come and give me your hand before I die'

DAVID RETURNED to duties in the Mediterranean during the early summer of 1800. The French army had stormed Alexandria in July 1798 and Sir Ralph Abercromby was put in charge of an expeditionary force of 14,000 men to retake the city.[30] In January 1801 the fleet assembled in Marmorice Bay on the Turkish coast just north of Rhodes. With the men of his company Stewart was on board the *Minotaur* – the ship he watched go aground at the mouth of the harbour of St Vincent a few years earlier – which was sent ahead to cruise off Alexandria and blockade the port.

Two enemy ships were taken – La Verte and *Polacco* – and David assiduously and successfully pumped information from the captured French officers round the captain's dinner table. A year later the Highlanders would receive a small amount of prize money for being present at the time of these engagements. Of the 152 soldiers on board the *Minotaur* about half were illiterate, signing their name with a cross. In their captain's hand 46 were marked as dead by the time the cash was disbursed.[31]

Part of a Sunday letter home to sister Jessie survives. David was writing on board ship somewhere off the Holy Land. He was living with Captain Louis, 'a man of fortune and lives as such'.[32] As so often, pestilence was raging ashore, preventing 'the pleasure of performing a pilgrimage to the Holy City and the temple of my namesake and his son Solomon'. In fact he would 'far rather walk into the Church of Fortingall or Weem next Sunday'. The surviving sheet is full of cheer, talking of a bet made with a fellow officer from Atholl that they would be home the following year. The loser would pay for 'a ball and Supper to twelve ladies and as many gentlemen of Tay, Tummel and Lyonside at Weem or Coshieville – only unmarried ladies or widows to be present, and the same restriction to extend to gentlemen'. He was careful to slip no hint about the operation in which he was involved.

The British force contained 12,334 effective troops. The French had 32,000 men as well as several thousand native auxiliaries. When the fleet reached Aboukir Bay, David reported to the Commander-in-Chief aboard the flagship and passed on the information he had gleaned from the prisoners. He then returned to the *Minotaur* and wrote a will. He left half his slaves and half the property he owned jointly with his brother John in St Vincent to his 'ever dear and truly esteemed sisters Clementina and Jess Stewart ... And in the hope that my West India affairs will prosper, I have the pleasure and delightful reflection of being of service to the most affectionate, dutiful and deserving sisters that ever a brother had been blessed with'.[33] His gold watch he bequeathed to William.

As David describes in the *Sketches*, on the morning of 8th March, some 5,000 British troops, including the 42nd, climbed down from their transports into open boats and rowed across a dead calm sea towards the shore. During the run in they were swept by grape and shells from the enemy batteries.

The French were waiting in the dunes above the beach and kept up such a fire that those in the boats 'compared the fall of bullets to boys throwing handfuls of pebbles into a mill pond'. To his chagrin Captain Stewart was not the first man ashore – he was third. The beach was firm sand protected from the artillery bombardment by the dunes where the enemy infantry was waiting.

Instead of launching an attack which would have cleared the beach, they allowed the British to land, draw themselves into two lines of battle and charge up the sand hills. Half way up the Highlanders came under fire from the muskets of the French dug in at the top. Eleven men of Stewart's company were killed in the first volley but the survivors were on the defenders with bayonets before they had time to reload and they fled. One commentator wrote that David Stewart 'by his gallant bearing and knowledge of the capabilities of his countrymen when properly commanded ... contributed essentially to the brilliant success which almost immediately crowned this daring operation'.[34]

Back on board the *Minotaur*, two of the captured French officers had climbed the rigging to observe, they said, 'the last sight of their English friends. But when they saw the troops land, ascend the hill, and force the defenders at the top to fly, the love of their country, and the honour of their arms, overcame their new friendship; they burst into tears, and, with passionate exclamations of grief and surprise, ran down below, and did not again appear on deck during the day'.

After the landing, Stewart pushed on into the dunes with two companies to drive back three field pieces which were 'galling the troops exceedingly'. His men were eager to keep chasing the enemy and he had some difficulty in making them rejoin the rest of the regiment which was waiting for reinforcements to land. David's best anecdotes, like what follows, are from footnotes to the *Sketches*.

'When the men laid down to rest after the action, I walked to the rear to inquire after some soldiers of my company who had fallen behind, being either killed or wounded. Observing some men digging a hole, and a number of dead bodies lying around, I stept up to one of them, and touching his temple, felt that it retained some warmth. I then told the soldiers not to bury him, but to carry him to the surgeon, as he did not appear to be quite dead. "Poh! poh!" said one of them, "he is as dead as my grandfather, who was killed at Culloden;" and, taking the man by the heels, proceeded to drag him to the pit. But I caused him to desist. The wounded man was so horribly disfigured as to justify his companion in the judgement he had formed. A ball had passed through his head, which was in consequence greatly swelled, and covered with clotted blood. He was carried to the hospital, where he revived from his swoon, and recovered so rapidly, that in six weeks he was able to do his duty. He lived many years afterwards, and was most grateful for my interference'.

In five days, Abercromby was ready and ordered a general advance from the beachhead. The action began against the French fortifications between the landing and Alexandria. The enemy attacked; the British beat them off and, harried by flying artillery – guns harnessed to six-horse teams – they advanced slowly across the desert.

Again it is footnotes to the *Sketches* that conjure up the battle. The 42nd had crept to within range of the foe and were hiding beneath a ridge as they waited for the order to charge. Three of the Highlanders could not resist popping up their heads to see what the enemy were doing. They were spotted; French guns opened fire and forced the Highlanders to retreat, leaving 13 men dead or seriously wounded. Of course David went back to help recover the casualties.

'One of the young men killed was of my company. A six-pound shot struck through both hips as he lay on the ground, and made a horrible opening as if he had been cut in two. He cried out, "God bless you, Captain Stewart; come and give me your hand before I die, and be sure to tell my father and mother that I die like a brave and good soldier, and have saved money for them, which you will send home." He said something else, which I could not understand, and dropping his head he expired.

'A strong instance of fear was at this time exhibited by a half-witted creature – one of those who, for the sake of filling up the ranks, although incapable of performing the best duties of a soldier, could not be discharged. When the regiment was again placed under cover, I returned back to the position they had left, with a few men, to assist in carrying away the wounded.

'After this was done, and the wounded carried off, I observed in a small hollow, at a little distance, a soldier lying close on his face, with his legs and arms stretched out as if he had been glued to the ground. I turned his face upwards, and asked him if he was much hurt: He started up, but fell back again, seemingly without the power of his limbs, and trembling violently. However

I got him on his legs, and being anxious to get away as the enemy's shots were flying about, I was walking off, when I perceived the surgeon's case of instruments which had been somehow left in the hurry of the last movement.

'Sensible of its value, I took it up to carry it with me, when I perceived my countryman standing up, having by this time recovered the power of his limbs. I put the chest on his back, telling him – in the hope that it would inspire him with a little spirit – that it would shelter him from the shot.

'At this instant a twelve pound ball shot plunged into the sand by our side. My fellow soldier fell down one way, and the box another; and, on my again endeavouring to get him on his legs, I found his limbs as powerless as if every joint had been dislocated. The veins of his wrist and forehead were greatly swollen; and he was incapable of speaking, and in a cold sweat. Seeing him in this plight, I left him to his fate; and, taking the case on my back, I delivered it to my friend the surgeon.'

The enemy retreated to their final defence lines in front of Alexandria. No way of breaking through these entrenchments could be at first discovered and the general withdrew to defensive positions before the city. The 42nd was placed on high ground to the right, adjacent to the large and magnificent ruins of a Roman palace.

Each morning Abercromby stood his men to arms at 3 am. On 21st March a musket shot and a cannon were fired from the French lines and the British knew that this would be a signal presaging an attack from their more numerous adversaries. The night was close, cloudy, still, and pitch black.

The enemy first engaged the right wing. The 42nd were split into two lines with a shallow valley between them. David suspected that the French might infiltrate the British lines along this hollow and ran out to reconnoitre.

In the darkness he could see no more than a couple of yards but he heard 'the murmuring noise of the movement of a great solid column, and the clank of their arms'. It was 900 men of the 'Invincible Legion', a crack French corps. He ran back to report to his colonel who immediately launched the regiment in a bayonet charge. The Highlanders on the opposite side of the depression turned and also attacked. The French rushed forward, straight into a British redoubt held by another two regiments. Two hundred and fifty Invincibles survived to surrender.

During this attack David's right arm was broken by a musket ball. 'In Egypt,' wrote a Gaelic poet years later, 'lead was placed in his arm'.[35] He also received a leg wound. Not being immediately disabled he stayed in command of his men until loss of blood and shock overwhelmed him. Even then he refused to allow himself to be carried to the rear. He stayed, propped against some stones, closely observing all that followed.

The enemy concentrated their attack on the palace ruins, known to the troops as Ptolemy's Temple, that the British had turned into a redoubt. The Black Watch were ordered into these fortifications but the command did not reach all companies. Those left exposed were spotted by French cavalry who immediately charged. The only defensive positions were some holes dug for cooking fires which offered slight impediment to the horses.

The convention of warfare was that infantry who had not formed a square would turn tail and run when attacked by mounted troops who would easily cut them down. Instead each Highlander stood his ground and met sabre with bayonet. The cavalrymen who swept through the line were cleared from their saddles by the regiments to the rear although a couple of stragglers nearly caught Sir Ralph who was saved by a corporal of the Black Watch. The French then attacked the isolated soldiers with infantry who were repulsed. Next they launched another cavalry charge with the same result as their first. British reinforcements arrived to support the decimated defenders in time to meet an all-out assault by General Menou's army.

It was now 8 am and the whole British line was under attack. Stewart describes cannon balls which skipped across the desert, removing a file of men at each bounce. The repeated assaults were repulsed and the enemy retreated, the last shots being fired at 10 am.

The city subsequently surrendered and French troops withdrew from Egypt. The 42nd had played a crucial part in the battle and captured the eagle standard of the Invincibles but six officers and 48 men were killed and 261 wounded. In the midst of the conflict Sir Ralph Abercromby was mortally injured. He was hit in the groin by a ball which lodged in his hip but he had continued to direct operations and only a trickle of blood down his leg revealed his wound.

In the *Sketches*, David devotes a couple of pages to the remarkable career and heroism of Sir Ralph but, as usual, it is the footnote that is irresistible. It lies at the end of a long description of the distinguished members of Sir Ralph's family and shows on what close terms Stewart had been with the Commander-in-Chief and his venerable father.

'I happened to be in Edinburgh in May 1800, and dined with Lady Abercromby on the day Sir Ralph left her to embark on that expedition from which he never returned. A King's messenger had arrived from London the day before, and Sir Ralph, only waiting for a few family arrangements, set out on the following morning. When at dinner with the family after his departure, I was affected in a manner which I can never forget, by the respectable old gentleman's anxiety about his son, and the observations and inquiries about his future intentions, and what service was intended for him. His particular destination was not known at that time, but it was suspected that he would soon be immediately employed. "They will wear him out," said he, "too soon," (the son was then in his 68th year,) "and make an old man of him before his time, with their expeditions to Holland one year, and the West Indies the next; and, if he would follow my advice, he would settle at home and take his rest." And when Lady Abercromby observed that she was afraid that he must go abroad, "Then," said he, "he will never see me more." The verification of this melancholy prediction was to be expected from his great age, being then in his 97th year. He died in the month of July following, eight months before his son, whose absence he regretted so much.'

David recuperated on Malta and returned to England with the regiment. The 42nd, and himself, were now heroes. He collected his first awards when the Turkish sultan Selim III ordered gold medals, the Order of the Crescent, to be struck and issued to all the officers who took part in the campaign. The Highland Society of London presented him a medal to commemorate 'the distinguished, brilliant manner in which the 42nd acted at Alexandria, under Sir R. Abercromby'.

The King expressed a wish to see the regiment and along with the Prince of Wales and the Duke of York reviewed the Highlanders at Ashford. David recorded that 'His Majesty was graciously pleased to express himself satisfied with the appearance of the regiment, but I believe many of the spectators were disappointed. There is no reason to suppose that good-looking men, more than others, suffer from the dangers and fatigues of a soldier's life. In the instance of the 42nd regiment, however, this was certainly the case; and although the men looked like soldiers, and wore their bonnets and every part of their dress, with a military air, they had a diminutive appearance, and complexions nowise improved by several year's service in hot climates. Some of their countrymen who were present participated in the general disappointment. They had formed their notions of what the 42nd should be from what they had heard of the Black Watch'. At the head of these ferocious little brown men, David must have looked entirely at home.

Nursed by his two sisters, he spent three months completing his convalescing at Drumcharry. He did not waste his time – he never wasted his time – instead he began to study and collect the history and traditions of the old Gaelic culture amid which he grew up and now observed beginning to succumb to Lowland and British civilisation.

In this he found an ally. James Irvine was tenant of Ringam, the tiniest of the Garth farmsteads with six acres of arable land set high on the hill overlooking the confluence of the Tay and the Lyon. The youngest of his six children, Alexander, was contemporary with David at the school in Fortingall and he personified that great Scots cliché, the 'lad o' pairts'.

Probably subsidised by *Fear Ghart*, he went on to St Andrews University and became a minister. His first job was on Islay and, in 1799, he became the missionary at Kinloch Rannoch which was two hours' walk over the hills from Fortingall. When visiting home, he would sometimes stay at the mansion house of Drumcharry rather than in the dank cottage that was his birthplace. In 1802 Irvine produced a book, *An Inquiry into the causes and effects of Emigration from the Highlands and Western Islands of Scotland, with Observations for the Means to be Employed for Preventing it*' and, doubtless, he and David spent evenings discussing the problems the Highlands faced in the modern world.

Stewart rejoined the regiment when it marched on into Scotland to be feted. Soldiers of the 42nd writing home or returning from the wars had carried his reputation to every glen. He had been the first — nearly the first — ashore in Egypt and was a wounded hero.

His biographer in the *Dictionary of Eminent Scotsmen* says at this stage of his career: 'He had studied the Highland character thoroughly; had made himself the brother and confidant of the men under him; and could, with an art approaching that of a poet, awaken those associations in their bosoms which was calculated to elevate and nerve their minds for the perilous tasks imposed upon them.

'The Highland soldier is not a mere mercenary: he acts under impulses of an abstract kind, which none but one perfectly skilled in his character, and has local and family influences over him, can take full advantage of. The usual principles of military subordination fail in his case; while he will more than obey, if that be possible, the officer who possesses the influences alluded to, and will use them in a kind and brotherly spirit. Captain Stewart appears to have enjoyed and used these advantages in a remarkable degree, and to have possessed not only the affections of his men, but of all connected with them in their own country'.

In 1803 David was given the formidable task of receiving the conscripted men of the Army of Reserve from the Highland counties and to form them into the 2nd Battalion of the 42nd

Regiment in Fort George. Altogether he enrolled 1,343 reluctant soldiers. The muster point for nearly 50 of them, three quarters speaking only Gaelic, was Perth.[36] These men were selected by ballot, a consequence of the Militia Act which had caused such chaos in Strathtay a few years earlier.

Entrepreneurs had been selling insurance to those liable for this form of recruitment and the young men of Highland Perthshire were keen customers. David ruefully remarked that this drained badly needed cash from the country and meant that most of those who arrived in answer to the summons were men enlisting for the money paid them by the insurance companies to replace the principals. To control this desperate bunch, the captain had one subaltern and a couple of NCOs.

According to the Act the recruits were to be paid a 'marching guinea' when they reached the official place of assembly at Fort George. Between there and Perth was a more than a hundred miles with little opportunity to obtain supplies on the way. Some of the recruits had already been given their guinea by the deputy lieutenants of their districts with which they could buy food to sustain them on the march northwards. Others had not.

The mutinies in several Highland regiments in the 1780s and '90s always had some recognised injustice at their root. With his understanding of the character of the Highlander, Stewart was well aware of the danger. The men were angry and undisciplined.

John Caw, the Provost of Perth, feared they would go on the rampage and loot his city and no troops were available to maintain order. The Provost, the Sheriff-Substitute, and David had a meeting and the latter came up with a solution. He would take out credit himself and lend a guinea to each man who had not already been paid, receiving back his money when the government gold was issued at Fort George. This pleased everyone and Stewart marched his recruits north without losing a man through sickness or desertion and not so much as a single hen was stolen along the route of the march.

Captain Stewart had acted without authority in lending this money, thundered Army Headquarters from Horse Guards. He was given a reprimand, read out in General Orders before every reserve regiment in the country. Always assiduous in corresponding with his betters, David sent out a few outraged letters and support came flooding in.

Provost Caw was 'quite astonished ... In place of being reprimanded you ought to have got a step of promotion'. He said that the Duke of Atholl 'has taken up the matter most keenly'. Caw and the Sheriff were to draw up a statement of the facts and the Duke would lay it before the Commander-in-Chief, the Duke of York. The Deputy Governor of Fort George also chipped in and, from Horse Guards in December, came the response that 'His Royal Highness doubts not that due consideration will be paid ... to the explanation you have transmitted to him [which] adduced of your general good Conduct upon that Occasion'.

The promotion to major came in 1804. If an officer could not pay for his new rank when it was offered he could recruit soldiers in lieu. For a majority the number required was ninety, for a lieutenant-colonelcy a hundred. The Highlands had already been scoured by recruiters, and some of those who were to join Stewart as officers in the newly formed 2nd Battalion of the Ross-shire Highlanders, the 78th, had great difficulty in raising their quota.

David went to his home strath. *Fear Ghart* was friend, adviser, and host to every man in the district and David's praises were sung by every invalided soldier coming home. The available men on *Fear Ghart*'s estates were already in the 42nd but in three weeks 118 men from the Perthshire Highlands had come to sign up at Drumcharry and another 30 or 40 had to be turned away.[37]

Stewart was always close to his family, particularly his sisters. The elder, Clementina, had the occasional romance but remained unmarried all her life and was often involved in her brother's later projects. During David's sojourn at Drumcharry a secret romance was maturing between Jessie and Alexander Irvine. Even though a minister was a gentleman, this youngest son of her father's tenant was always conscious of the great social gulf that existed between himself and the laird's family. Before David would come home again, Irvine would be appointed minister of

Fortingall, and two months later, in the only unconventional act of his life, he and Jessie would elope and marry.[38] Their friends were astonished. *Fear Ghart* was incandescent with rage but, although he remained icy towards his son-in-law, he learned to accept the liaison. To David, the minister already was and would remain a confidant and trusted friend.

CHAPTER SIX

Maida

'The Pride of the Presumptuous Enemy was severely Humbled'

IN FEBRUARY 1805 the 2nd battalion of the 78th embarked at Fort George for Hythe in Kent. In June David and four lieutenants were ordered to India to join the 1st battalion. He was the protagonist in the events which followed, although in this footnote in the Sketches he does not identify himself.

'The day before the field-officer fixed on for this purpose left the regiment, the soldiers held conferences with each other in the barracks, and, in the evening, several deputations were sent to him, entreating him, in the most earnest manner, to make application either to be allowed to remain with them, or obtain permission for them to accompany him. He returned his acknowledgements for their attachment, and for their spirited offer; but stated that, as duty required his presence in India, while their services were at present confined to this country, they must, therefore, separate for some time.

'The next evening, when he went from the barracks to the town of Hythe, to take his seat in the coach for London, two-thirds of the soldiers, and officers in the same proportion, accompanied him, all of them complaining of being left behind. They so crowded round the coach as to impede its progress for a considerable length of time, till at last the guard was obliged to desire the coachman to force his way through them. Upon this the soldiers, who hung by the wheels, horses, harness, and coach-doors, gave way, and allowed a passage. There was not a dry eye amongst the younger part of them'.[39]

The upshot of this extraordinary incident was a petition to the Commander-in-Chief from General Moore. The Duke of York cancelled the transfer and ordered David to return to the battalion 'in which he had so many friends ready to follow him to the cannon's mouth'.

In 1805 the 2/78th was shipped to Gibraltar, passing through the wreckage left by the Battle of Trafalgar. There David was appointed by General Fox to introduce a uniform drill to the garrison. In May 1806 the 78th sailed for Sicily which, with Naples and southern Italy, had been united since the eleventh century as the Kingdom of the Two Sicilies. King Ferdinand was a Bourbon, son of King Charles III of Spain. After Nelson's victory in the Battle of the Nile, Ferdinand declared war on France. After various vicissitudes, he was ousted by Napoleon's brother Joseph and fled to Palermo, which was under the protection of a British garrison. Its commander in Sicily, Sir John Stuart, decided on an invasion of the mainland and asked for additional troops. His army landed unopposed at the Gulf of St Euphemia but the British soon encountered the French commanded by the experienced General Reynier and the Battle of Maida ensued.

In the *Sketches*[40] Stewart paints the engagement in vivid detail. It took place on 6th July 1806, a hot day in the midst of harvest. The field was totally obscured by powder smoke after the first volleys. Wadding from the soldiers' cartridges set the ripe corn ablaze and some of the French wounded were burned to death. Twenty years later David decided he and the other surviving officer of the 78th, James Macdonell, deserved a medal from King Ferdinand and this is part of the account, possibly written by the latter, which was produced for His Majesty.

'The disparity of numbers was considerable; the British force being 4750 men and 60 Artillerymen with three small field pieces; that of the French 7500, with 300 Cavalry and a train of Artillery. The field of battle was an open plain with an even surface, offering no obstruction to the advance of either side.

'Both were drawn up (each in two lines) in the centre of the plain. The first line of the enemy from their superior numbers extended considerably beyond both flanks of the British front line, which consisted of three corps – the Light Infantry Battalion on the right, the 78th Highland Regiment in the centre, and the 81st

Regiment on the left; the whole amounting to 2150 men. – The French first line of 3900 men was drawn up in a similar and parallel order directly in front of the British, and at the distance of about 600 yards.

'Leaving the second line, consisting of the Grenadier battalion and the 27th Regiment, considerably in the rear, the first line commenced the attack by a forward movement in slow time till within 300 yards of the enemy, when they rushed forward in double quick time, charged with the bayonet, and drove the French back to within a short distance of their second line. After a short pause, to allow the soldiers to recover breath and to reform the line correctly, they charged again, and with such effect that the first line of the enemy was driven back on the second, and both being intermingled retreated in great confusion, but endeavouring to rally and offer an opposing front, they were again charged and driven back with great loss.

'At this period the British second line marched up and formed on the left of the first line, when the whole advanced; and charging the enemy with increased vigour, compelled them to retreat in such irretrievable disorder, that, despairing of being able to make any further resistance, they threw away their arms, and fled with a speed which could not be overtaken, sustaining, however, a loss of 930 men killed, and 1146 so severely wounded that they could not leave the field, besides a number of slightly wounded who escaped to their rear, while the loss of the British was only 1 officer and 41 Soldiers killed, and 11 officers and 269 soldiers wounded, being in the proportion of 30 killed of the French to 1 of the British.' [41]

It was not quite so straightforward and David's actions that day singled him out as possessing remarkable moral as well as physical courage. In his record of military service David describes his own part in the battle. 'In this Action I had an opportunity of performing an important piece of service – Personal attachment and regard for the memory of Officers whose Character might suffer by my stating the particular circumstances of this affair, prevent me from doing so – I have had the same feeling from the day of the Battle; and I not only have avoided writing on the subject but even speaking of it except to those who were present and knew the whole.

'It was from this feeling that I requested of Sir John Stuart not to mention the circumstances in his Dispatches, although he was very desirous to do so in justice to me – He was also fully sensible of the great and important piece of Service rendered to him; which turned on the point whether to be a victorious or beaten general; to prove a forerunner and a good sample of the reverses which the French afterwards sustained.

'Actuated as I have always been by a delicacy towards the memory of my friends, who are dead, I cannot now enter into a detail of circumstances and only state generally that, by a prompt and decided interference I checked a retrograde movement (more properly a retreat) of my regiment in the very heat and most important moment of the Contest; which would have left the centre of our Line clear for the Enemy to pierce through – Thus taking each of our wings in flank and in front – movements for which General Reynier was fully prepared – our Troops so exposed could not withstand the Shock and would with ease be driven off the field before the second line could come to their assistance.

'The proposed Retreat of my Regiment, which would have had such deplorable consequences, proceeded from a misapprehension of Orders, the confusion of the Officers who carried and delivered them, and from other causes which need not be detailed. – How quickly our brave young Soldiers recovered from the panic with which they were struck, when they saw themselves running away from those who had previously fled before them with terror and precipitation, was soon proved by their rapid and irresistible charge on a veteran Enemy so much more numerous.

'Immediately after this Charge which completely overturned an Enemy who from the previous movement had calculated on no resistance and an easy conquest, I was wounded, but, being able to walk, I kept the field till all was over; and then, as at Alexandria, had an opportunity of observing every movement and event during the subsequent part of the Action'.[42]

Stewart added a little to this in a private memorandum written for King Ferdinand in 1828. He noticed that the 81st Regiment, next in line, was not acting according to plan so he rode over, had words with their colonel, and made him rectify the situation. When he returned to the 78th he found the Highlanders disengaging from the line of battle and preparing to withdraw. Both officers and men were young and untried. The retreat had been triggered by the appearance in the French lines of a formation with a very similar uniform to a regiment on the British side. The soldiers' fire had slackened and then confusion piled upon confusion.

'Surprised at this unexpected movement, he asked the cause, when the Commanding Officer informed him that he had received orders to retreat from the field. Seeing that he was determined to obey the orders as he conceived it to be, and was proposing to march to the rear, Major Stewart hurried away to the General Commanding the Brigade, and begged him to recall the order ... The Brigade General answered that he had given no such order, and that there must have been some mistake.'

David instantly rode back to his regiment. One must imagine the roar of guns, the cries of the wounded and powder smoke lying like a thick fog across the battlefield. The Commanding Officer, Lt-Col Patrick McLeod, was wounded in the battle and he may have already been out of action. Many of the officers had lost their heads trying to organise the demoralised withdrawal and this was infecting the men.

This was precisely the type of situation for which Stewart had been drilling the men since their induction into the regiment in Scotland. His instruction had continued in Kent under that master of training troops, Sir John Moore, and in Gibraltar where he had charge of disciplining a corps comprising all the light infantry in the garrison. David knew how quickly and unquestioningly the Highlanders would obey his orders. And he knew that action to rectify the situation must be immediate.

He never wrote down the details of his 'prompt and decided interference' but he told his family, and the story was later recorded. To stamp his authority on what was in danger of becoming a frightened rabble he shot one of the hysterical officers and immediately re-formed the regiment, ordering the men to open fire on the foe as soon as their muskets would bear. 'So correct and deadly was the aim of our young soldiers, that in ten minutes the field in their front was cleared of the Enemy. Thus the misapprehension or mistake about orders turned out to be highly advantageous; and Major Stewart learned afterwards from a French Officer, that it was considered by them as an able manoeuvre or ruse from which they suffered most severely'.[43]

David's wound which gave him trouble for years afterwards was to the right arm that had already been injured at Alexandria. It took him a year's leave of absence, spent at Drumcharry, to mend. One suspects that he would have been an honoured guest round every peat fire and in every laird's house in Highland Perthshire during his recovery. He never again regained full use of the limb and taught himself to write with his left hand. In consequence his neat italic handwriting descended into an idiosyncratic script – dashed off at great speed – which John Prebble described as 'an Oriental pattern of curves and whorls, heavy strokes for the consonants and a light feather touch for vowels'.[44] David himself was always aware of its inadequacies and it can be utterly impenetrable.

An anecdote on the subject survives from the early 1820s. 'Sandie Proudfoot, the old Keltneyburn carrier, had on one occasion to tell him that the Perth merchants could not read the orders from Garth he had taken to them, but the answer was – "O don't believe them, Sandie, for figures are enough for them"'.[45]

Although strategically unimportant, Maida was the first time that Napoleon's soldiers had been defeated in continental Europe, and the public hailed it as a mighty victory. Maida Vale in London commemorates the action. In 1808 the King issued a gold medal – 'the first action for which medals have been granted by His Majesty to the officers of his Army'[46] – which was awarded to David and 16 other senior officers present.

The Patriotic Fund at Lloyds presented him with a silver rose bowl inscribed 'To Major David Stewart of the 78th Highland Regt. In testimony of his Gallantry and Judicious conduct at the Battle of Maida, on 4th July, 1806 In which the Pride of the Presumptuous Enemy was severely Humbled and the Superiority of the British troops Gloriously Proved'.

By the beginning of 1808 David had rejoined the 2nd battalion of the 78th stationed in Canterbury. On 21 April he was promoted to Lieutenant-Colonel of the Royal West India Rangers. Before he left, his brother officers dug deep into their pockets to present him with a magnificent gift in the form of a Highland broadsword, its elegant basket hilt of silver instead of iron. Commissioned from London maker Josiah Johnston, it is unique. Before this date a few silver-hilted broadswords exist but are almost exclusively associated with kings and princes. Later in the nineteenth century a few more were made but they are all heavily ornamented – costume jewellery rather than a real weapon like this. On each side of the basket is a parcel-gilt escutcheon. One carries the motto and badge of the 78th and 'Maida', the other the arms of the Stewarts of Garth. Amongst the extensive etching on the blade is an inscription recording that the sword was presented to David by 'his brother officers as a testimony of their high regard and esteem for him as an officer, companion and friend'.

The wording of the affectionate inscription goes well beyond what is usual on such presentation objects but the lavishness of the gift must be an indication that his fellow officers knew that David had saved the honour of the regiment at Maida and, by extension, their own reputations and careers. The weapon was lost after the recipient's death but it turned up recently in a Geneva saleroom and in 1998 the National Museums of Scotland, judging the sword important both for its merit and for its association with David, bought it for the nation.

Lieutenant-Colonel Stewart sailed for Barbados where he took command of his Regiment and the island's garrison of more than 3,000 men. This was no ordinary appointment. Any soldier deemed incorrigible by the army was either executed for his crimes or transferred to the Rangers for life. The sentence rarely lasted very long. If the enemy did not kill a man soon, the fever surely would. The day before Stewart assumed command, 36 men had been flogged. In the previous eight months, 307 men had deserted, 295 had died of disease and the 'unprincipled depravity exhibited by two thirds of the Men was horrible'.[47]

Their new commander was 36 – small, balding, bespectacled, with a crippled arm held in a sling. That was not his only problem. In 1809 he wrote to Major Robert Dick, a Perthshire man who had fought with the 78th at Maida, from Barbados. He was 'free from sickness but not free of pain for I have been deprived of the use of my leg for these seven weeks by a violent pain from the wound I got at Alexandria in 1801'.[48] He had to miss a chance for more glory in an expedition to Martinique. Perhaps he felt it necessary to belie his appearance at once. Four men were due to be flogged for shooting at their officers. He had them face a firing squad instead. In the early days of his command another two offenders were shot and three more hanged.

'It would be inconsistent with the brevity of these memorandums,'[47] wrote the colonel in his record of service 'to explain the means by which I endeavoured to reclaim and reform these men, to check crimes and desertion, and by new habits of regularity, and change of Manners, to prevent the occurrence of diseases incident to dissolute and intemperate depravity. I shall therefore only state the result as was seen in the conduct of the Soldiers.

'By punishing with the last severity when necessary, but preventing by every possible endeavour the commission of Crimes; encouraging and rewarding every symptom of improvement; so contented with their Situation, and so regular had the Men become, that during the last eighteen months I had charge of them, desertion had disappeared, the number of deaths was reduced to the usual proportions in that Climate – Punishments were very unfrequent, and then only quite slight; and altho' quartered in an open Barrack, in a populous neighbourhood, with many objects of temptation, there was not a complaint from any Inhabitant against a Soldier during a period of eleven months, and thus their conduct proved the gratifying change in their habits and principles.

'By this contrast which I witnessed in the Command and direction of Soldiers in two Corps of a high scale of moral rectitude; and of other Soldiers without principle and debased by many vices; my own knowledge of human nature was increased, and many new lights afforded me for discovering the best modes of preserving the primitive habits and character of good men, and of improving the dissolute and hardened'.

As well as turning military dross into gold, David had one opportunity to add to his battle honours. In 1810 he commanded a Light Infantry Brigade on the expedition which captured Guadeloupe. It was attached to the division commanded by Major General Harcourt, who, after the failure of an attack he had ordered on the principal post of the enemy, said, 'If I had employed Colonel Stewart on this Service, I would have had the happiness of seeing Guadeloupe conquered and the Garrison surrender to the Troops under my immediate Command'.[47] This earned David another medal – the Peninsula Gold Medal 1806–9 with a Guadeloupe bar.

From Barbados, he and his regiment were moved to Trinidad. There peace reigned and Stewart was all too aware that careers were being made elsewhere whilst he was stuck in this West Indian backwater. But, as he told Robert Dick, now fighting in the Peninsula with the Black Watch, life was sweet. 'Except for Athole this is the most beautiful country imaginable ... The roads are excellent and I am well mounted and have provided myself with a smart gig for Sundays ... On the 4th June I danced till 6 in the morning, on the 5th rode 15 miles to dinner and home at night'.[49]

In a later letter to Dick he expressed the frustration that underlay his idyll. 'Idle as I am here and without professional duties sufficient to fill up one fifth of my time I endeavour to find out such pastimes as are best suited for occupying my mind and keep me from idleness which of all is to me the most oppressive and fatiguing of all situations.'[50] He was determined that no opportunity for advancement should be overlooked.

CHAPTER SEVEN

Career in Suspense

'I am too old, stiff and grey, and none of the young girls will look at me'

IN 1810, Lord James Murray, second son of the Duke of Atholl, married a daughter of the Duke of Northumberland. From Trinidad, David wrote to Lord James to congratulate him.

'Accustomed as I have ever been to look up to the family of Athole with respect and affectionate esteem, thus imbibing with my mother's milk the feeling of my forefathers, it was with a pleasure consonant to such sentiments I lately heard of your marriage, on which I now, in unison with all those men of Athole who feel as I do, beg leave to offer my heartfelt congratulations on a circumstance that must afford satisfaction to every friend of the family. May you, my dear Lord, with your fair Bride be as happy, honourable and prosperous as I so sincerely wish you, and sure am I your measure will be complete'.[51]

It is a long letter. Murray was influential, an M.P., and his correspondent was aware that the wars against Napoleon must come to a close and the prospects for a short-sighted, disabled officer, however distinguished his career, would not be particularly bright in a greatly reduced peacetime army. David wanted a job in colonial government.

He told the bridegroom that he had sent a case of tropical birds as a wedding gift and hoped they would escape the depredations of 'those sharks at the Customs House'. He intended to send a live flamingo in spring. He described the beauties of Trinidad, the studies he was making of its natural history and offered to send any other specimens Lord James might desire.

As well as occupying himself in roving the island, David was to return to Britain with 1100 preserved examples of the island's fauna and a similar quantity of specimen plants in his baggage to present to museums and botanical gardens.[52] He had told Dick he had discovered enough 'as would fill a little volume'. He would later become a member of the Linnean Society. In the letter he continues, describing the social and political set up of the island.

The colony was split between those who favoured English laws and those who preferred the old Spanish law. David avoided taking sides because his duty wass to protect them all. 'I have done my best to bring the people together ... and we have set some social and merry meetings on foot, and this cohesion and inter mixture seems to have the best imaginable effect in sweetening the sourness caused by their bickerings and heartburnings, and disputes about laws, jurisprudence and such subjects as I am sure they do not understand. In this sociability the Militia take the lead in allowing of nothing but that which promotes happiness and harmony, and my corps and myself have got into great favour with the people, black, white, and all shades of colour and complexion. Of the latter indeed there is not much in this climate, the vermilion of the ladies not being of that showy brightness which makes my Flamingo look so gorgeous as he stalks with his awkward gait among the fowls'.

To Robert Dick, David explained that he hoped to become Governor of the island. 'The situation is in itself honourable and worth nearly five thousand pounds sterling a year. This is too much for my interest' — which meant that his friends and patrons did not wield sufficient influence to obtain such a post for him — 'and tho I now wait an answer I dont expect a favourable one. I am not ambitious of power but I am ambitious of showing my respectable and good father and my family and friends that in a community such as this divided and differing on almost all other points — with regard to me and my qualifications for their government — they are as one. This my father will see and with this I am satisfied and a negative to the application will be no disappointment to me'.[50]

To impress one's father is a common motivation for advancement, particularly if one is forging a career in a field of which he would have little understanding. More unusual, and typical of David Stewart, is to express this to a friend with such artless candour.

David was acting Commander-in-Chief on Trinidad and had organised the erection of a statue to General Thomas Dundas, a much respected administrator of the island until his death in 1794.[53] The governor since 1803 was General Thomas Hislop who had commanded a division in the Guadeloupe campaign. After leaving the island he would win a baronetcy and more glory in India. He had clear ideas as to his successor.

'Government House 6.6.1811. My Dear Colonel I know not when I sat down with more pleasure that I now do in compliance with the wishes and requests of many respected inhabitants of this Colony to convey to you my opinion and the desire of this Community that you should succeed me after my departure for England; on this subject you know already my sentiments, but I cannot avoid repeating how much I wish you to be my successor ... Therefore as an officer and as a member of Society, with your taste and zeal in the discovery of natural productions of the island and the agreeable improvements you have suggested, and which have been acted upon, it is with warm wishes and hope that I anticipate the success of your application and with great regard'.[54]

The salary of a governor was £3,000 per annum and, in a good year, this could be doubled by fees received in the secretary's office. In 1815 the Governor of Curacao said that he had saved £8,000 in just three years.[55] In pursuit of the position in Trinidad David wrote to the Duke of Atholl at Dunkeld House, just across the Tay from the Irvines' manse at Birnam, asking for his support. The supplication was sweetened by a case of stuffed birds. The custom sharks disembowelled them and, by the time they were received at Dunkeld, Sir Ralph Woodford was already the new governor and David had left the island.

In a letter which caught up with him months later in London, Her Grace assured David that she, the Duke, and her son Lord James Murray did 'every exertion in our power'[58] to obtain the

Governor's post for Stewart. Rather embarrassingly Woodford's father was the Duke's closest friend but the Duchess writes that the first they knew of the appointment was when it was announced.

The letter ends on a note of mild panic. 'Your sister Mrs Irvine mentioned a great many other Birds you had been so kind as to send to me, but which have never come to hand, it is vexatious after your trouble, and I have to entreat you not to send any more, as we are more than satisfied with the fine specimens you have sent us which have arrived and we all beg to return our sincere thanks for your kind attention in thinking of us, the birds are the surprise and wonder of all that sees them'.

The problems of patronage must have prevented the entry to heaven of many a bigwig. The first their Graces knew about Woodford's appointment may have been when it was announced – but the Charter Room at Blair Castle contains a letter from Sir Ralph in which he states 'how gratefully sensible I am of the strong terms in which you were so good as to name me to Lord Bathurst'.[57] Bathurst was Colonial Secretary and the Governorship of Trinidad was in his gift.

Colonel Stewart returned to Scotland at the end of 1812. He was 41 and unemployed. After only a month's inactivity in the depressing company of brother William and his father at Drumcharry he mounted a white horse and went on a tour of the north of Scotland, staying with the myriad connections he had made in his years of service with the Highland Regiments, and making more.

David's charm is revealed in the warm terms that people wrote to him and about him. Words such as beloved, kindly, sympathetic are applied and, although he was always properly impressed by his social superiors, he had a great gift for friendship and for mixing with people of all classes and ages.

His interest in the culture of the Gael had been inculcated in him in boyhood. He had made extensive use of his understanding of the Highlander during his service career and now he began to take notes about what he saw and heard in his travels. When he returned to Drumcharry, he wrote to Jessie's husband, Alexander Irvine, telling him that the Duke 'hoped it would be so managed as that I could succeed Sir R Woodford ... I must remain in suspense – Whatever way the business ends I have in no small degree served myself in making great People in London believe, as I am told they do, that no man would so succeed in embodying a Corps as I can do – whether the belief is well founded or not is a different thing – it is so far to my advantage that it is believed – this is not the first time that a man has got credit where perhaps it was not due'.[58]

The remainder of the letter concerns domestic matters and David, as always, is full of sound advice and the common sense on which he prided himself. Irvine was minister of Little Dunkeld which had charge of Strathbraan which stretched west from Dunkeld towards Amulree. The district was still largely Gaelic-speaking and the minister was much respected by his parishioners. In the Sketches Stewart described him as 'a conscientious, able, and zealous clergyman'.[59] He and Jessie had a young family and David advised him to take in the sons of the gentry for instruction so that his five boys made contacts useful to them in later life.

David also discussed a new circular saw that had arrived at Inver, a mile north of Dunkeld, and asked the minister to look at it. 'If it is the same as is lately come into use in London for sawing veneers. I wish to send some special timbers for a trial of the execution of this instrument'. He had brought exotic woods back from the Indies and these, put through the Inver saw, were probably the origin of a cabinet at Drumcharry House which had doors veneered in irregular concentric circles of tropical woods. It appeared in the salerooms in the 1960s and was described by one observer as 'a truly hideous piece of furniture'.

Stewart was in London, at 70 Pall Mall, by September 1813 with a new scheme which had received general approval from the powers that were. For the time being he shelved his hopes of becoming a Governor in the West Indies and now intended to recruit himself a regiment, calling it the Athole Highlanders, for service in the war against the United States in America. He wrote to Alexander Irvine asking him to keep his eyes and ears open for any potential officers who must be able to bring their own men to the colours. David also asked for approaches to be made to the local sergeants of the militia to discover if they had any likely lads who would join him. After all they need not fear 'such hard fighting as they have had in France or Germany, judging by the specimens we have had of Yankee soldiership'.[60]

The last time the Athole Highlanders had existed was in 1783; they were disbanded after their mutiny. It is a measure of David's reputation both at Horse Guards and in the straths of Perthshire that it was considered feasible that he should be able to recruit a new Highland regiment. In 75 years of warfare 50 battalions of Highlanders had been raised, the last being the 93rd Sutherland Highlanders in 1803. Normally only a chief or a member of a chief's family could command the allegiance in a district that would ensure the young men would join the colours of a new regiment. No mention is made of the Duke's patronage. That surely would have been requested later.

Stewart goes on to thank the minister for offering to lend money but his plan is thought so good that he should not need any. 'I cannot help thinking that my Father might come forward with a lend of some hundred pounds – and more than a lend I do not require – the old gentleman does not seem very willing to part with his money, and I do not think he will say I have ever bore very heavily upon him – indeed by looking about among his neighbours he will find severals of them whose sons have been more expensive to them than I have been to him, and this without having preserved that appearance in the world and society that I wished ever to sustain'.

Alexander Irvine had literary ambitions. He was an authority on Gaelic, his first language, and collected poems which are a rich source for modern scholars. In 1802, after leaving Islay, he had published his inquiry into emigration which is still quoted in works on the Highland Clearances.

As well as his best sermons, he left unpublished and unpublishable manuscripts which included a 'State of the Highlands in 1809' and a description of the Vale of Fortingall. Like many such works of the period, the latter is maddeningly useless to the modern researcher. 'Behold the Lyon foaming with rage between two rocks – the sound of its streams is that of defiant thunder' is a typical sentence. The minister even wrote a romance which a kind parishioner – Mrs Izett, wife of the King's hatter who had bought the estate of Kinnaird – told him was embarrassingly bad. Perhaps to teach himself humility he destroyed this manuscript but preserved the critical letter.

In 1810 he received the patronage of the Highland Society of London for a plan to produce 'The Lives of Caledonian Bards', but it was never published. In 1817 he was made an honorary member of the Society, its highest accolade.

Later Irvine and Stewart's sister Clementina would be the chief critics of the Sketches, the Presbyterian and Whiggish principles of one being balanced by the Episcopalian and Jacobite beliefs of the other.[61] 'When I have fifty pounds to spare,' wrote David to his brother-in-law, 'I intend to employ it in paying some intelligent persons to collect old anecdotes of the Times of our Forefathers and of their feuds publick and private – and all such – old Kindrochet [James Robertson, laird of Kindrochet at Struan, four miles west of Blair Castle] could himself fill a volume of Athole anecdotes alone – Robert McArthur's wife for Glen Lyon, others for Breadalbane and so on. When I am settled at home wanting a leg and an eye this will be a good amusement'.

Wellington's army entered France in October 1813, which made it increasingly unlikely that the new regiment would be formed and Stewart began to think seriously of producing a book. In February of 1814, he wrote to an old friend with whom he had kept up a correspondence since 1800, Captain Duncan Robertson, the heir to Kindrochet. He had fought his way up the Peninsula and was then in France with his regiment, the 88th, the Connaught Rangers. David asked him to 'please tell Mr Stewart with my good wishes that while I am extremely sorry for the death of his brother ... I now feel his want as I am anxious to set on foot a literary work for which he had a turn, and would have given great assistance in the execution of this plan'.62

The letter ends on a personal note. 'Malcolm Stewart, Brother to Shierglass [an estate opposite Blair Castle in Strathgarry] is dead in Jamaica, so that if you and your old sweetheart Miss Sophy Stewart make up matters, you and yours may be Lairds of Shierglass, for I see no prospect of Shierglass marrying ... I would have you not delay too long like me, till I am too old, stiff and grey, and none of the young girls will look at me, and those of my own standing such as my old flame Miss Flemyng are something like myself – we have seen better days, and you are now in your prime, so don't lose your time and opportunity'. Captain Robertson took his friend's advice and the old sweethearts were wed in 1816, but the Shierglass estate succumbed to debt and their offspring were never its lairds.

CHAPTER EIGHT

Unemployment

'For to me nothing is more oppressive and fatiguing than idleness'

BY THE BEGINNING of April 1814, ever restless, the old warhorse took himself off to France on the frigate Venus. Napoleon abdicated on 6th April; Marshall Soult was beaten after a sharp battle at Toulouse on the 10th by which time Stewart was already in Bordeaux. He wrote to the Duke of Atholl on the 11th.

'Last night and the whole proceeding the town and neighbourhood was in a blaze of illumination, and wherever a party of English officers appeared the people crowded round them clapping their hands and waving their hats in the air and cheering, and crying out "the brave English, our friends and deliverers from tyranny to our liberty and legitimate government!" Last night as I was walking with the Honble Mr Bathurst of the Guards and some other officers, an old lady in the excess of her joy and happiness came up to Mr Bathurst, embraced and kissed him exclaiming "the English are the favoured country of heaven and you are one of the angels!" and it was some time before Mr Bathurst got clear of her embraces'.[63]

The 42nd had distinguished itself at Toulouse where its Commanding Officer, Robert Macara, was wounded. David no doubt visited him for they had been at school together in Fortingall. Stewart also discussed the battle with the victorious general Lord Hill, another old comrade – this time from the attack on Alexandria – and obtained a different perspective on the conflict when he paused by the roadside near Carcasson where a French infantry brigade was on exercise. After inspecting the troops, he talked over the campaign with their commanding general.[64]

In spite of his activity, the colonel must have known his fighting days were over and he remarked to a friend when he was back at Drumcharry later that summer that 'this peace for which we have been praying and fighting for so many years is a severe check [to careers]'.⁶⁵ He goes on to talk about marriage. 'I could never muster the courage and I do not find at this time of day that my bravery is at all improving. I was delighted some time ago with a report that we were to have Miss Betsy for a neighbour – but I suspect that this spoken of match was something in the stile of my match making – always getting the consent of one side – that is my own, as I suppose the case with the gentleman in question – but never finding the way or means of getting the consent of the other party'. Granted David was neither rich nor handsome, but one would think he would have been an entertaining, if exhausting, husband.

He spent the summer travelling in Scotland. In June, he was made a brevet colonel and placed on half-pay of 8s 6d a day which, combined with the substantial pension of £62 10s a quarter he received for his wounds, gave him £405 2s 6d a year, a modest income befitting a gentleman. In October he presented a petition to the Duke of Atholl, laying out his credentials and asking for the Duke's patronage to obtain an appointment. It is one of the most revealing documents of David's that survives.

'As a natural consequence of the state of the world my situation in life is coming to a crisis,'⁶⁶ he begins. He faces a choice. He could return to the West Indies to command his old Regiment which 'would be the cause of surprise to many who perhaps think too favourably of me'. There follows a 600 word exposition of the methods he used to transform his regiment of reprobates into disciplined soldiers – but 'I cannot but think I should be lowered in the opinion of the world were I again to join this Corps'.

His alternative is 'being reduced to ... idleness – which of all others is that I most dread and dislike, for to me nothing is more oppressive and fatiguing than idleness – Now, My Lord Duke, seeing how I am situated, and my case being as it were desperate I ... intreat your Grace's support in the only prospect ... I now have to save me from that retirement and listless mindless oblivion which I am so anxious to avoid, for when a man is active and in publick, if he cannot much benefit himself, he may at all events serve his friends'.

He wants a job in the West Indies and reminds the Duke of the support he had from the colonists which was not given because of his 'servility or humouring their prejudice (of which I hope I am incapable and would heartily despise myself for such)'. He then produces an anecdote to illustrate how he gained their trust. 'Sometime after I arrived in the West Indies seeing how numerous Desertion had been, and being always more anxious to prevent the commission of rather than punish crimes, and observing that one great cause was the encouragement Deserters met with from the Inhabitants who harboured and employed them on their Plantations; therefore while I endeavoured to keep the men occupied with exercise amusement and some employment or other, I published in the Newspapers my determination to enforce the law against such as I would find harbouring soldiers.

'I waited till I got full information against two of the principal and most conspicuous men in the Island (for to punish a poor Rogue or man of colour would have been disregarded and considered as a thing of course). I got Warrants to apprehend them which I was obliged to enforce by using some strong language to the Attorney General of the Colony who was not much in the habit of criminal prosecuting white men, and sent an officer and Party along with a Constable to bring them in to procure Bail to appear at the next Sessions.

'The whole Colony was in an uproar – Such a thing was never heard of – to bring gentlemen – White men – Members of the assembly in by force like so many slaves and Negroes – what was to be done? I had taken my resolution and was determined to shew perseverance in what had begun till at last these gentlemen fully acknowledged their fault, and the President and Members of Council asked me as a favour to give up the prosecution and save these men the consequent disgrace of trial and Conviction, and they, promising for themselves, and the Colony every assistance in seizing Soldiers and prevent harbouring them, I immediately complied.

'The result was that in twenty two days ninety five deserters were sent in to the garrison from the Country, and even afterwards when a soldier appeared straggling in the Country instead of being protected and paid as formerly, all were up in chase of him – black, white and all colours – hunting him from Plantation to Plantation till at last he was obliged to take shelter in the very place he had left in the Barracks ...

'My military duties coming in the course of time so easy, I employed my spare time in visiting and examining not only every quarter of Trinidad both cultivated and uncultivated, but also several of the neighbouring Colonies. Paying particular attention to all the principal objects (so much that many imagined I was taking a survey of the Islands not believing that a man would take so much trouble and apparent fatigue for his amusement) and mixing much and freely with the people, I acquired a considerable share of knowledge of the peculiar habits and character of the Inhabitants, Black as well as White, with such a proportion of all that is interesting to know of a Country that I have well authenticated accounts and returns of the Produce – number of pounds of sugar, coffee and cotton and Gallons of Rum with the number of Negroes with those born and dead and quantity of Cattle etc etc for the last five years on the Islands of Trinidad Grenada St Vincent and others. This not only of the Islands in general, but the amount of produce and increase and decrease by Births and deaths among the Negroes of almost every estate.

'What I more than anything else attended to was the treatment, comfort, and health of the Negroes on the different plantations and the various changes and improvement in the comfort and happiness of the Negroes. I also busied myself in suggesting such improvements as would not only lessen the labour for the Negroes, but increase the produce of the Planters.

'One great and important instance of this was prevailing on some sensible men to attempt the Plough, all Field work being performed in that Country by the hoe and the hand. They got some Ploughs and Harrows out from Scotland and I gave each planter two soldiers who had been accustomed to the Plough at home to teach the Negroes.

'I had the satisfaction of seeing after much perseverance and many difficulties in overcoming prejudices and the like, on a fair trial one Plough and two horses turn up as much land as eighteen Negroes did in the same time. This was proof to the senses, and before I left the Island eleven Ploughs were in full operation altho I much fear that stubborn prejudice will prevent persevering in this system.

'Such with others too long to notice here, are I believe the causes of the desire expressed by those People, and as I find my constitution unimpaired and being ready to encounter any climate and all privations and difficulties for a proper object, I am emboldened by that kindness which your Grace has ever shewn me, and for which my gratitude is such as I can more easily feel than express, to say that my present object is to be appointed Lieut Governor of Trinidad, so that I might carry on the Duties of the Government in the absence on account of health or otherwise of Sir Ralph Woodford, whose judgement, decision and excellent regulation in his Government have been such as would render the task of his successor easy in following his example.

'Could I hope for your Grace's support and recommendation to Lord Bathurst on this, or any other appointment in the Colonies, that the last wish of my heart would be to shew my gratitude by my exertions to prove myself deserving of such countenance ...

'I will be supported by men and parties who might be supposed to have opposite principles but each of them have done me the honour to say that as they know no man whom they would have no more pleasure in seeing appointed to a situation of authority in the Colonies such as would afford the means of forwarding the prosperity of the Country, and more particularly the happiness and welfare of the Black Population.

'These were Mr Stephen the member with his friend and brother-in-law Mr Wilberforce who, hearing of me in some manner I know not how, applied to me for information on the State of the Negroes with a number of queries, and at the same time requesting me to suggest such improvements as I thought would tend to ameliorate their condition. On these subject I have had several conversations with Mr Stephen, and I believe I may assure myself of his cordial support.

'The other parties are Mr Marryot the Member, agent for Trinidad and other Colonies, and a great proprietor and West India Merchant with others of the same Body who appear to form the same opinion as Mr Stephen and as they think that a Governor with the inclination has much in his power to promote the happiness and prosperity of those under him they pay me the compliment to express a desire that I should have such an appointment at the same time offering their support'.

David heard that the Governorship of Grenada had become vacant and requested the Duke to intercede on his behalf with the Prime Minister Lord Liverpool and, in November 1814, again asked for help in obtaining a more humble appointment, that of Barracks Master in Barbados. Nothing came of these and only one more time would he ask for help from this quarter. He had expected the Duke, the natural patron of his own family, to exert himself on his behalf. It appears that this was not the case and his relationship with the dominant family of Atholl was henceforth circumspect.

At the beginning of December 1814 David was in London on half pay, still hopeful of an appointment, and on the make. He had attended his first meeting of the Highland Society of London as a guest of its Chairman in February 1814 and joined as 'a Highlander born'[67] before going to France the following month. This body had lobbied to have repealed the proscriptive laws against Gaelic culture imposed after Culloden and, when the ban on Highland dress had been lifted in 1782, sought to promote and preserve the culture of the Gael through sponsoring piping contests and Highland games, collecting and publishing Gaelic poetry and folklore, and a Gaelic dictionary. Now patronised by the royal dukes, the Society was a lairds' club, counting many

Highland aristocrats amongst its membership, and they formed a slice of the nation increasingly anglicised and remote from the people who once formed the backbone of their wealth and power. At the January 1815 meeting of the Society David was appointed a vice president and, on 10th February, he joined the committee to organise the management of the Caledonian Asylum which had been founded to assist indigent Scots in the capital. Fellow members included Sir John Sinclair – a great agricultural improver who produced the incomparable Statistical Account of Scotland begun in 1791 – the Earl of Breadalbane, Captain James Hamilton, the chairman, soon to be secretary of the Society, and John Galt, second only to Walter Scott as Scotland's most influential writer. Like Scott and David, Galt had the knack of making influential friends. Stewart returned to Perthshire at the end of the month, but his restless energy was soon put to work for the cause.

CHAPTER NINE

Tartan

*'To him the Society was indebted for the idea of collecting
the Tartans of the different clans'*

WHILST AT DRUMCHARRY during the winter of 1814, David received a letter from the fashionable miniaturist Andrew Robertson suggesting that 'Tartans, Plaids, and Banners' of the clans ought to be preserved. The Highland culture was much in vogue at the time. From the obloquy that followed the '45, about which a correspondent of the colonel's remarked that 'it became fashionable by all ranks to run down the name of Stewart which must be a real slur on a civilised nation on cool recollection',[68] the situation had been transformed.

James MacPherson's Ossian, whether forgery or not, had taken Europe by storm, even being carried on campaign by Napoleon for bedside reading. Then came Dr Johnson's *Journey to the Western Isles*, the heroism of Highland soldiers in the wars (which many seemed to see personified in the battered little form of David Stewart), and the romances of Walter Scott.

Stewart knew Scott – the first surviving communication between them dates from 1811[69] in which David suggested buying up and publishing books in Spanish since the expected freedom of the colonies in South America would mean 'the Spanish language will be much cultivated throughout Europe particularly by the British'. He was to collaborate with 'The Wizard of the North' more than once during his life.

The colonel enthusiastically took up Andrew Robertson's idea, and revealed himself to be already expert on such lore. 'There are several heads of families who are not chiefs,'[70] he replied to the artist, 'but who have distinguishing marks and plaids and banners, such as Lord Breadalbane, head of a powerful branch of the Campbells, Glengarry, Glencoe and Keppoch of the Mac-Donalds, and so on.

'There is no proper Stewart tartan, unless what is called Prince Charles Tartan be considered as such. There is a painting of Prince Charles in a Plaid, and Tartan coat in this house for which it is said he sat when in this country in forty-five. I shall take this with me to London as a specimen.

'Besides the Tartans of chiefs, and heads of families, there are country and district Tartans, such as the Athole Tartan (of which there are two kinds both very beautiful, one for the Plaid and Coat, and Kilt, and one for the Hose and trouser). These are considered as the Tartans of the Country, and not of the family of Athole. There is also the tartan of the Country, of Breadalbane, Lochaber, Badenoch, and many others'.

The truth about the origin of Highland dress is obscure. It first came to national prominence after the Union when opponents chose to clothe themselves and their families in tartan of any and every description to show their Scottishness. The Jacobites took it on as a badge of their identity and, save for its use by the Highland regiments, it was subsequently banned for nearly forty years. In 1815 that most preposterous of Highlanders, Alexander Macdonell of Glengarry, formed his Society of True Highlanders. In 1822 he listed a gentleman's full Highland kit which members were expected to wear.

'A belted plaid and waist Belt, a Tartan Jacket with T.H. buttons & Shoulder buckles, a scarlet coat TH^{rs} Cut with TH^{rs} Buttons, A cocked bonnet with Clan Badge and Cockade, A Purse and belt, A Pair of Highland Garters, A Pair of Hose, A pair of Highland Brogues (with whangs) and A Pair of Clasps to Do for Court use'. Along with this went the arms. 'A Gun (or Fusee) with a sling, A broad Sword and Shoulder Belt, a Target and Slinging Belt, A Brace of Highland Pistols and belt, A 'core Dubh' or Hoc knife called the "Skian", a powder Horn with Chain or Card, a short Pouch and cross shoulder belt'.[71] He missed the dirk, the eighteen inches of cairngorm-encrusted kitsch with its built-in knife and fork but his list captures the pantomime nature of the full Garb.

The codification of tartan had not been considered before although as soon as it was mentioned it seemed obvious – but not to everyone. David first wrote to the chief of Clan Donnachaidh, Col Alexander Robertson of Struan, at the west end of Loch Rannoch. The answer came back 'More than twenty years ago I wished to ascertain what the pattern of the Clandonachy Tartan was, and applied to different old men of the Clan for information, most of whom pretended to know what the pattern was, but as no two of the descriptions I received were exactly similar, and as they were all very vulgar and gaudy, I did not think proper to adopt any of them'.[72]

One suspects Struan had hit the nail on the head. Tartans were gaudy – that was their point – the gaudier the better because a good loud red had once required rare and expensive dyes and signalled wealth. It was a symbol of status for what seem to have been garments most used when travelling. But, although some case could be made for district tartans where the natural dyes available in any neighbourhood would be reflected in its product, of clan associations there was little sign. David told Andrew Robertson about it. 'A few more years as you justly observe and the memory of such things will be lost, and the truth of this cannot be a stronger proof than that Strowan does not properly know what his own Tartan is'.[70] It does not cross the colonel's mind that the memory may not have been so much lost as never having been there at all.

Enthusiasm was one of his most endearing characteristics, and sometimes rather overwhelming, as shown by his gifts of birds to the Duchess of Atholl. A similar reaction comes from Struan in a delicate allusion which would have passed David by. He had offered the old chief and the other large proprietor in Rannoch, Sir Neil Menzies, help in establishing a post office at Kinloch. 'We are both under great obligation to you,' wrote Robertson, 'for having had the goodness to assist us, which, along with many other instances evinces your desire of being serviceable to your friends, as well as your being at times more capable than they are themselves in accomplishing their wishes'.[72] If Struan's response contains a hint of affectionate irony he was not alone amongst the colonel's correspondents.

David took time to send Captain Simon Fraser a few melodies for his *Airs peculiar to the Highlands and Isles of Scotland* which was being published by the Highland Society but he was in full cry after tartan, dashing off letters to the chiefs, seizing an excellent opportunity to network amongst those before whom he would like his name to be prominent.

The McNab who, like Glengarry, was painted by Raeburn as if posing for his shortbread tin had the information at his finger tips. He was 'highly honoured by your giving my tartan a place in your Collection. There are two other setts of it as worn by "The Houses of Acharan & Inishewan" Cadets of the family, the one considerably larger, the other a smaller sett, but this is the one mostly worn by me'.[73] David must have liked the 'your Collection'.

The Highland Society of London was to hold the register, each clan tartan to be authenticated with the seal of the chief. Along with the letter from James Hamilton asking for each chief to supply his sample came a round robin from the President, the Duke of Kent, asking them to sign a Loyal Address to the Prince Regent.

In September 1815, when Napoleon was halfway to St Helena and the war finally over, Stewart was made a Companion of the new military division of the Order of the Bath, awarded only to senior officers who had distinguished themselves in the field. The colonel proudly devised for himself a coat of arms combining those of the Garth and Kynachan families with his new medal dangling beneath. It was most irregular and never registered with the Lord Lyon but he had it engraved on his spoons and used it on his seal.

His old arm wound was giving him trouble that winter and he retired to Drumcharry to be nursed by Clementina. His friends wrote in concern at the news. Col Alexander Stewart, retired surgeon of the 73rd Regiment, recommended Dr Alexander Robertson in Perth. He was an old friend of David's and had been a surgeon in the Egyptian campaign. He had 'a steady hand and a firm mind like your own. He will make a bold opening on the part which has distressed you for so many years, if the arteries will permit it. You can have no difficulty in getting him to Drumcharry, which will save you the pain of the journey'.[74]

It seems that David had osteomyelitis, a chronic infection of the bone marrow of his injured arm which was not infrequently a consequence of wounds before antibiotics were developed. Typically this would flare up at intervals and require an incision to be made through flesh to the bone which would be scraped to allow the build-up of pus to escape. The pain during these episodes and the pain of the operation would be dulled by laudanum. The wound would require frequent changes of dressing while it drained and smelled foul.

During his recovery David continued to deal with the tartan registration. Some of the replies were sent to London but many came to him at Fortingall. Like the McNab, Lord Ogilvie could give precise details.[75] Other chiefs had not the faintest idea of their clan patterns but promised to do their best to find out and forward examples. This often meant copying one of the designs shown in an old family portrait. Others denied they ever had a tartan of their own and still others proudly claimed the government sett used by the 42nd for the best part of 80 years.

Colonel Robertson of Struan, an old friend of both Stewart and Alexander Irvine, whose first-born was the chief's nameson baptised Alexander Robertson Irvine, still protested the erroneous assumption behind the scheme but did join in. 'It does not appear to be apertained, either by tradition or authentick history, that the different Clans in the Highlands of Scotland, wore any distinctive pattern or tartan. It is well known that they all had particular Colours, or Standards, emblemetical of some of their most honourable atachments, but as far as I have been able to discover, they wore no uniform Garb'.[76] Struan eventually produced a tartan scarcely seen since which bears no relation to the modern tartans of the Clan Donnachaidh.

What is remarkable is how many of the respondents knew the

colonel and tenderly asked after his health. More evidence of the extent to which he was known and appreciated by his fellow countrymen comes in a letter of spring 1816 from Alexander Campbell, a musician, writer and Walter Scott's former music teacher, concerning a project that David was promoting to the Highland Society.

'I have the satisfaction of telling you that the poetical and musical work you allude to is under preparation and a considerable proportion of it ready for the press. My principal coadjutor the learned, ingenius, & I may add great Walter Scott, our common friend, labours along with me two evenings regularly in the week – his zeal, nay his enthusiasm is eminently useful – he is the very soul of undertaking – he has composed some of his happiest numbers to several Highland melodies & others to Lowland airs hitherto unpublished – the words are admirably united with the exquisite simple music & as our object is to please we have reasonable hopes of not altogether disappointing they who retain a relish for native simplicity & the genuine offspring of the Scottish Muse'. Campbell ends with a reference to James Hogg, the Ettrick Shepherd. 'Mr Hog's friends expect him to Town in a few days ... I know he values you as one of his best friends – and I am not a little proud of your favourable opinion of, Sir, your most humble sert'.[77]

Glengarry wrote in typical style: 'I sympathise with your painful sufferings with all the warmth of a True Highlander who follows his Countrymen with a keen eye into every Field where Glory is to be reaped, and who has frequently rested it with satisfaction on your course in the Battles of our Country'.[78] He hopes David will be 'sporting your dirk at the Presentation of their Address by the Society of True Highlanders'.

David had attended meetings of the True Highlanders, which was composed of local lairds prepared to suffer Glengarry's eccentric and dictatorial leadership, but Alexander Macdonell already had his detractors. James Hamilton, secretary of the Highland Society of London, was not one of them. 'I like him very much, some Folks say he has a bee in his bonnet, but if he is mad, I wish to God he would bite some of his Brother chieftains and put into them a portion of that Spirit and Feeling with which he is animated'.[79] Although the chiefs were increasingly interested in the romantic trappings of their culture many of their tenants were leaving or being forced to leave their ancestral farms. During the previous three quarters of a century populations across western Europe had been growing fast, leading to growing pressure on the land. Then the revolution in agricultural practices swept through, dislocating the peasantry in country after country. Like Ireland, the Highlands were amongst the last places in Europe to feel the effect of these changes. Great efforts were made by, among others, the Forfeited Estates Commission and the Duke of Argyll to provide new enterprises in the region – such as linen, wool, and fishing, but only kelp proved a success until its market collapsed in the 1820s.

The improved agriculture led to higher rents and more profit to the proprietor – and cut the requirement for labour. In England the need for Acts of Parliament to enclose common land gave some check to the landlord but Scots law gave no such safeguard. The lairds' power was absolute. The situation was further complicated by the beliefs of the Highland peasantry. Although the crown had been issuing charters to the chiefs almost as soon as the clan system came into being, the people still believed that the land was theirs, held in trust by the chief for the whole of the community.

In many instances the love of the people towards their chiefs was gone, driven out by alienation and exploitation. But sometimes old attachments clung on in face of seemingly insuperable odds. In 1843, a generation after David gathered material for his book, an Atholl friend of his, James Robertson, Sheriff Substitute of Tobermory on Mull, went aboard a shipload of emigrants which anchored in the bay. 'I spoke to one or two among them, one a Macdonald with all the old feelings of attachment to his Chief. – "If he had his own," said the poor fellow, "we would not have been here today". How unworthy of his position in life has this wretched and contemptible trifler proved himself; by his folly and vanity he has ruined an honourable people'.[80]

The apologia for the clearances was given by James Loch, who managed the affairs of the immensely coal-rich Marquis of Stafford and his wife. She was the Countess of Sutherland and inherited more than a million acres of that county.

In Loch's view the law was supreme. It gave the land owner the right to do as he pleased with his property and it was his duty to increase its productivity and profitability. The indigenous inhabitants were feckless, idle impediments to progress. The fact that they had lived on the estates for generations was irrelevant; the fact that they still looked up to their lairds as their chiefs and fathers was also irrelevant. If their dispossession should leave them destitute they were a problem for society as a whole, not for their dispossessors.

In rural England paupers were supported by the parish and the cost fell heavily on the backs of the proprietors. Not so in Scotland. In the Highlands the able-bodied poor must survive by beggary and the generosity of their neighbours with no cost to the laird. But when he cleared a district all became destitute. This philosophy and its results were directly contrary to the old patriarchal values taught to David Stewart by his father. As a Gaelic poet said, *Fear Ghart* preferred people to sheep.[81]

The Clearances in the Highlands had been well under way since the 1780s. Those in Sutherland had begun in 1800. David had personally observed the troubles in Ross-shire during the Year of the Sheep in 1792 and his own travels in the north must have merely confirmed the reports he had been hearing from his soldiers to whom he was 'brother and confidant'. In the previous few years the parishes of Dornoch, Rogart, Loth, Clyne, Golspie, Assynt and Kildonan had seen extensive removals, and, in the most notorious clearing in the summer of 1814, tenants were burnt out of their homes in Strathnaver.

The colonel can have been doing little to endear himself to many fellow-members of the Highland Society when James Hamilton wrote in February 1816: 'Your last letter like many others is so interesting and contains so much important Matter on the political Economy of the Highlands that, in making my report of the Correspondence with you on the various views of the Society, I shall take the Liberty of introducing your remarks into the Minutes, that they may remain to posterity as wholesome and sound Advices, and be a lasting Mark of your zeal and patriotism. What a misfortune it is that the great Highland proprietors will shut their Eyes against evidence of the strongest fact'.[82]

In March Hamilton wrote again: 'Your Observations on the Management of Highland Farms coincides so entirely with my own, that, as mentioned in my last I shall ingraft them on the Proceedings of the Society. I read part of them to Lord Reay, and wish Lady Stafford could see them. The latter has published a pamphlet on the late great improvements on the Sutherland Estate. It appears to me to be written with the aim of palliating the Obloquy which she must be sensible attaches to her late conduct to her miserable Tenantry'.[83]

On the subject of the tartan collection Hamilton reports a vote of thanks after the Society's anniversary meeting: 'To Colonel David Stewart for the true Highland spirit, zeal and feeling evinced by him on all occasions, and for his judicious attention to the duties of Vice president. That to him the Society was indebted for the idea of collecting the Tartans of the different clans, and the success with which that interesting object had been hereto attended'.

David could not and would not take all the credit and ensured that Andrew Robertson's initial contribution was also marked in the minutes. The colonel was still at Drumcharry where his father and elder brother made it clear that they did not require his advice on how to run their estates. He was still recovering from the infection in his old wound and was concentrating on being fit for an important visit to Edinburgh.

CHAPTER TEN

Genesis of the Sketches

'I strongly advised him not to publish'

THE BLACK WATCH came home from the wars in March 1816 to the Edinburgh equivalent of a ticker tape parade. Carriages and pedestrians lined the route of their march from Portobello to the palace of Holyroodhouse. From there it took the regiment an hour and a quarter to march up the mile-long High Street through tumultuous cheering crowds and pealing church bells to the Castle.

At the head of the procession marched General Hope, commander of the Castle. Alongside strode David Stewart. Incongruous amongst the kilts he would have been in his Royal West India Rangers uniform with his medals bouncing on his chest, the wispy circle of fair hair round his balding head covered by his cocked hat and its fluttering plumes, his spectacles clamped to his nose, and his disabled arm resting on the hilt of his silver-hilted presentation sword.[84] Beside him was an old friend, the Regiment's new commanding officer, Robert Dick. He would succeed to the estate of Tulliemet, where the Tay joined the Tummel, a dozen miles from Drumcharry. In 1846, a knight and major general, he would be mortally wounded by the last shot fired by a Sikh gun at the victory of Sobraon.

Dick's predecessor in command of the 42nd, an even older friend, Colonel Macara, had been killed at Quatre Bas just prior to Waterloo. His father had been minister of Fortingall immediately before Alexander Irvine. David Stewart had kicked his heels alongside the young Macara through many of his father's sermons.

That evening the soldiers were given free tickets to the theatre and Walter Scott organised a public dinner for the officers. The latter misbehaved, drawing reproofs from their elders. David stayed on in lodgings in Frederick Street for a couple of months where he received a letter from Farquharson of Invercauld: 'I regret very much to learn that the Young Men of the 42nd exposed themselves in their conduct about the Waterloo dinner at Edinburgh. I am sorry to observe that there are many of the Officers of that Corps composed of very different men from those mentioned by you – their Correspondence on a former occasion with the Highland Society of London gave many wellwishers of the regiment greatest concern – injuries may be forgiven but insults admit of no compensation'.[85]

This last was a reference to a recent attempt by the Highland Society of London to honour the capture of a French 'eagle' at Alexandria in 1801. It had belonged to the Invincibles whose column had been spotted by David. Their standard had been surrendered to Major Stirling of the 42nd but the sergeant to whom it was entrusted had been stunned by a horse and when he recovered the eagle was gone. Another eagle mysteriously appeared in the possession of a soldier of a different regiment who claimed to have captured it from a French cavalry officer.

The Society asked for enlightenment from the Black Watch officers. They decided the regimental honour was being questioned and returned an intemperate reply and it was left to David to broker a peace.[86] Col. James Stewart of Urrard, another retired officer of the 42nd from Highland Perthshire, mentions the public vilification which the regiment had received and he also makes it clear that his old comrade was already collecting material for a book.

In the introduction to the *Sketches* the author states that not until 1817 did the Duke of York ask him to take on the task of writing a history of the Black Watch but it was high in his mind at this time – one way of occupying himself until he could obtain a proper job from the government. In February 1816 Urrard had written: 'It will be a delightful occupation to retrace the path you formerly pursued in the Black Watch ... Assisted as you will be by your celebrated friend, you cannot fail of doing justice to your subject. But, my good friend, fearless as you have always been of the consequences when prompted by high sense of duty, do you apprehend no danger from blazoning the deeds of the Royal Highlanders at the conclusion of a War which has placed so many fine feathers in the Caps of other Corps well known to entertain no slight jealousy of yours? If you are resolved to brave all the obloquy that must attach to this task of giving printed notoriety to the valorous achievements of your compatriots in arms, let me recommend due consideration of the materials that you are to submit to your friend, who deals so habitually in fiction that he may not be disposed to submit to the drudgery of confining himself to trite prose'.[87]

Walter Scott was already the most famous Scotsman in the land and yet it appears that he was willing to put aside his prolific pen to assist the colonel in the preparation of his military annals. At that time it sounds as if David was to submit the results of his research to Scott who would then write it up. National pride and honour would be won by a good history of the Royal Highland Regiment and this would have been close to Scott's heart but one suspects that favours are being exchanged.

Scott was in the midst of writing *Rob Roy*; Stewart had listened eagerly to the stories of men who had known the famous cateran – the grieve on Kynachan had been his close henchman. In the *Sketches* David would write a seven page essay on the outlaw[88] as well as proving himself the great expert on old Highland lore. Scott could not have had a better source of material, stored in a mind as romantically inclined as his own. To be the original of Baron Bradwardine was claimed by half the gentry of Scotland but *Fear Ghart* surely must have a better case than most.

Unlike many travellers to the Highlands who intrepidly ventured amongst the savage inhabitants to report upon their quaint and primitive habits, the colonel was one himself with command of the language and a deep love and understanding of Gaelic culture. But its economic foundation was facing increasing pressure. The close of the Napoleonic Wars led to the collapse of farm prices, the end of the injections of soldiers' pay, and intensifying land clearances.

Stewart began to rove the Highlands to gather material for his book, using the same meticulous methods of inquiry that he had perfected in his examinations of the islands of the West Indies. He was talking to old soldiers to fill gaps in his skeleton history and he soon discovered that he was gathering enough material to extend his work to encompass all the Highland Regiments. If the memory of the veterans could not stretch back far enough, that of their widows often did since many had followed their husbands in the campaigns. In the *Sketches*, the author – inevitably in a footnote – describes an attack in St Vincent in 1796. A man in David's company had been ordered to stay behind to guard his comrades' knapsacks but his wife did otherwise.

'When the enemy had been driven from the third redoubt, I was standing giving some directions to the men, and preparing to push on to the fourth and last redoubt, when I found myself tapped on the shoulder, and turning round, I saw my Amazonian friend standing with her clothes tucked up to her knees, and seizing my hand, "Well done, my Highland lads," she exclaimed, "see how the Brigands scamper like so many deer!" – "Come," added she, "let us drive them from yonder hill."' [89]

One of David's notebooks survives from the time that he was carrying out research. Its thirty sewn pages, nine inches by three, are covered with his most casual and illegible scrawl, filled in at random. At one end it begins with a note of work carried out by tenants at Drumcharry. At the other it opens with the phrase 'The Argyle men more partial to the sea than the land service'. The pages are filled one way and then the other. Even in mid page the writing will suddenly be upside down or across.

This is a typical sample of those jottings, mostly *aides memoire*, that are decipherable and coherent: 'Mrs Macdonald Bell's Wynd – Nothing makes a man so brave as there being no danger – 1794, Ross, 437 & 1809 Ross, 768 – Coloured negroes good troops under their master, good for nothing under officer – Spring Circuit of 1762 there was no prisoner for crime of debt within the counties of Kincardine, Aberdeen and Banff – Nobody would speak to me but to curse me for betraying my prince – Ingratitude is a word unknown in the Gaelic language – Memorandum to prevent repetitions – Many wounds got in odd places – 25th April Capt Hodgson, dinner at half past five – 15 July £13 in desk, 18s in pockets – Thos Prentice at Kilsyth, the first man in Scotland who planted potatoes, died in the year 1792. This appears in the transactions of the Royal Society – Mr Lockhart Thursday dinner – Lady Abercromby, dinner half past five – Write to Lewis Grant esq St Vincent about Alex Robertson, mason – Trees of the largest size found 1500 feet above the limit of the sea – improvement of small tenants costs little – Surgeons of Highland regiments should always speak English – The morality of the Scotch more owing to what they hear from the clergy than on what they read – In the town of Peronne in Picardy close to the church there is a tree of great magnitude which appears from the original grants for building the church dated 661 to have been full growth at that early period – The present system is to refuse the lower orders of all permanent property, everything that would make a man believe he has a stake in the country – At Preston the Highlanders pulled off their bonnets and ejaculated a short prayer, I know not if the educated civilised soldiers of the present day are so mindful – Forced to beg for work destroys a man's spirit'.[90]

Stewart stayed with fellow members of the gentry, smoothing his passage with curiosities collected in the West Indies. His generosity could be overwhelming. Lord Kinnoull described his gifts as 'lavish'[91] and said that he would only keep them in trust for the donor. His ambition for his work had further expanded by the spring of 1817, still before the Duke of York's request for a history of the 42nd.

The character of the Highland soldiers had been unique in the army. They considered crime dishonourable; punishments were virtually unknown and their courage, courtesy, and decency was recognised by both friends and enemies. In recent years the quality of recruits had degenerated insofar as their use to the army was concerned. Stewart set out to describe the society in which these men had been nurtured and the reasons for the decline. He knew already of course. He had witnessed the Year of the Sheep and the people of the Highlands would have told him their fears because they trusted him. These were the families of the soldiers who had wept when he left Portsmouth.

In Edinburgh at some time during this period, David met Elizabeth Grant of Rothiemurchus, who wrote a sketch of him. She was about 20 and he was in his mid-40s. 'I had an old lover all to myself,'[92] she wrote, 'unshared with any rival, won, not by my bright eyes, but by my spirited fingers, from playing the highland marches as Lady Huntly had taught me them. Old Colonel Steuart of Garth, seventy, I should think, always in a green coat, and silver broad rimmed spectacles, was writing the history of the 42nd Regiment, and the slow Black Watch, and the quickstep of the Highland Laddie, given better, he said, than by the band of his old love, so over excited or over enchanted him that he hardly ever quitted my side, and he gave me his precious work on its publication. I had my two thick volumes too, but they were not heavy ones. He was a fine old soldier, though a little of a bore sometimes, so very enthusiastick about the deeds of his warrior country men. He never went further in his love making than to wish he were a young man for my sake, so that Jane had the advantage over me of a real offer'.

David went down to London the following spring, settling himself into writing the *Sketches*. He wrote to his brother-in-law from rooms in Duke Street telling him that 'I purpose giving up this idle round of dissipation, and to take a small retired lodging in the neighbourhood within reach of the Library and apply with heart and zeal to the compilation of the military annals of the Highlands'.[93]

He responded with anger to news from Alexander Irvine that His Grace had appointed a new factor who was likely to clear old tenants. The Duke 'is running the same race of avaricious oppression and ignorant infatuation which is so quickly driving so many land holders to their ruin. Although I am not altogether in opinion with the people, so many of whom firmly believe that a heavy judgement and retribution will fall on such grinding oppressors, I am clear of opinion that they will deserve a judgement and punishment who in their hunting for profit and increased incomes showed no pity for the suffering of others, nor cared what became of them, and drove them from their possessions with as little feeling as they did their cows and sheep when sent to the market'.

Living quietly, with only a few forays into Scotland, David spent the next three years in the capital writing the 350,000 words of the Sketches. Towards the end of 1819, he asked the Duke of Atholl one last time for help in obtaining a job. He heard that the Governorship of one of the West Indies had been offered to two officers who had turned it down. He was unhappy that it had not been offered to him and he was now eager for crumbs. A minor post was vacant on St Kitts which was under the Governor of the Leeward Islands. Would the Duke approach the Foreign Secretary, Lord Bathurst, on his behalf? [94] Answer came there none.

Just before returning north in March 1820 he was asked to look for a position for a young relative by Sir John MacGregor-Murray, chief of the MacGregors, whose son was married to Lady Elizabeth Murray, daughter of the Duke of Atholl. David wrote back stating that jobs were hard to come by, but he would do his best. He went on to say that his 'heart and blood was chilled when I read the whole of Athole to be laid waste agreeable to the advertisements in the Perth papers ... I dreamed for two nights of the misery and perhaps consequent actions to which these outcasts – the moral, the brave, the industrious men of Athole – will be subject to when driven from their ancient homes'.[95]

David was not prone to hyperbole. What he wrote was what he thought, or did. He would have had two nights of bad dreams about the fate of the people with whom he felt so closely identified. Sir John wrote back to deny the truth of these reports, saying that it was simply that tenants were not reapplying for leases.

In replying to Sir John, Stewart accepts that he was misinformed and that 'You and I coincide most cordially in a most perfect attachment and respect for the Duke of Athole'.[96] He writes about

1. Colonel David Stewart of Garth CB. Probably painted in London in 1817 when he was writing the *Sketches*. He is wearing the uniform of the Royal West India Rangers and sporting his new medal – Companion of the Most Honourable Order of the Bath. (*Private collection*)

2, 3. Compare this caricature of Stewart by Caroline Norton with the cover. She – the self-portrait is also from her commonplace book – was a Sheridan by birth, and a poetess 'distinguished for her beauty and wit'. Her husband's family owned estates in Atholl and Rannoch but the marriage failed amid great scandal and she gained a reputation as a feminist by fighting for her rights.

4. John Stewart of Garth by Sir Henry Raeburn, painted in 1823 when the sitter was over from Trinidad to extract money from his elder brother and deposit on him an illegitimate daughter.
(*Private collection*)

5. Jessie Stewart of Garth, wife of Rev. Alexander Irvine. Photographed before her cottage door in Pitlochry, she was the last of the 'kindly Stewarts of Garth'.

6. Stewart's medals, except his CB. Only 17 Maida medals were awarded, the first ever given by the King to officers in the Army. The miniature was probably painted around 1790 while Stewart was an ensign in the Black Watch and stationed in Scotland.

7. The silver sword, also shown on the cover, presented to Major Stewart by his fellow officers. One gilded escutcheon shows the arms of the Stewarts of Garth, the other an imitation of the shoulder plate belt of the 2/78th with the regimental motto and the battle honour 'Maida'. *Courtesy of the National Museums of Scotland (Scottish United Services Museum) (M1998.29; A4937, A4938).*

8. John Murray, 4th Duke of Atholl, the great Highland magnate, did not use his enormous influence to promote Stewart's career, suspecting him of having 'Radical tendencies'. Stewart, at one point, described the Duke as a 'grinding and cruel oppressor' and wished to insert an account of his 'deplorable doings' in the London newspapers. From the collection at Blair Castle, Perthshire.

9. Landing of troops at Aboukir Bay, by Philip James de Loutherbourg. Stewart wished to be first ashore. To his chagrin he was third. The fall of shot in the dead-calm sea was described as being like 'boys throwing handfuls of pebbles into a mill pond'. Reproduced by courtesy of the Scottish National Portrait Gallery.

10. 'Here and there a white knee betrays a Soutron or Lowlander – in most the limb is as dark as that of Glune-dhu (Black Knee) himself'. Urban Highlanders eyeing each other's kit during George IV's visit to Edinburgh. By Sir David Wilkie. Reproduced by courtesy of the Scottish National Portrait Gallery.

11. Statue of David Stewart erected on the old Garth estate at Keltneyburn in 1925. Jimmy Shand played at ceilidhs in front of it.

12. Governors' corner in the military cemetery on St Lucia. David Stewart lies beneath the obelisk. The grave is still in good repair.

his concern, having heard that 5,500 were being removed from the Lovat estate and others on Novar, a Munro property in Sutherland. He moves back to Atholl and the dismissal of the factor. 'As Capt Stewart, a most judicious honourable country gentleman who declared that he could not in good conscience follow up the measures proscribed, was dismissed, and a man totally ignorant of the people, their language, their character, their habits, the history of the country, its produce and its soil – a man totally ignorant of all these was employed in preference to an honourable humane country gentleman whose object was to do justice to landlord and tenant. With all these I am sure the Duke would consider me very impertinent to interfere. Mr McDiarmid refused the farm in Glengarry when he found that 25 families were to be turned off in June, several weeks after the legal term of agreement'.

In the fifteen inches of shelf space occupied by the 7th Duke's mighty *Chronicles of Atholl and Tullibardine Families*, in which there is no reference to any clearing, the change of factors is mentioned. 'Mr Frederick Graham ... was appointed the estate factor in place of Captain James Stewart, who had proved incompetent'.[97]

The colonel cites other parts of the quarter of a million acres of the Atholl estate where the old inhabitants had been turned out. 'All the tenants from Rotmell to Tullymet, the same for the wood of Inver to Dalguise, all in Glentilt and the neighbouring glens. I mention the 24 families on the farm of Strathgarry. And it is needless run over all the estate of Athole'.

Sir John prevaricated but Stewart was not having it. 'Is not the clearing away of the inhabitants of a whole district and giving their lands to Lowland farmers extirpation?'[98] And he pulled no punches when it came to Macdonell of Glengarry in whose Society of True Highlanders Stewart had been involved, but now he was scathing. 'Glengarry farms contained 1500 souls. Those farms have now 35 persons. Is not this extirpation? and yet Glengarry with a consistency only to be equalled by the rest of his character goes about the country attending public meetings and making speeches in his own praise as a true friend to the Highlanders'.

Stewart returned to Drumcharry with his manuscript almost complete. He was looking forward to the dinner of the Celtic Society, of which he was a co-founder, in Edinburgh and told Sir John that 79 gentlemen had attended the last, almost all in Highland dress. He was to bring a copy of the controversial section of the book down to the dinner to leave with Sir John to get his opinion. The letter has MacGregor-Murray's response on its back. 'MS second part which I read over & found to be of such a nature that I strongly advised him not to publish'.[99]

David was attacking the ruling class, his own. This was the behaviour of Radicals who that spring were exploiting the distress of factory workers laid off on account of the severe weather. Cavalry were in action to control the disturbances. In September two of the leaders were to be hanged and their bodies decapitated. In spite of Sir John's disapproval Stewart stuck to his guns. "Notwithstanding I must continue to think my opinion correct. [The system] I do think cruel, oppressive and destructive to the best and true interests of all'.

At the same time he was conscious of the pressures upon the longtime land holders facing a declining market for the produce of a Highland estate since the end of the war. He cites examples in Highland Perthshire. 'Macnab and Lude are gone. [Colonel John Robertson of Lude was to drown himself in August in the River Tilt a day or two after quitting his house], Struan hangs by a thread, which his death will break – Ballechin has got £29,000 in marriage portions and legacies – has sold £11,000 worth of lands – and is still running up new debts – my father and brother were on the same path, but I hope they are stopped – all this is very melancholy'.[96] He was to discover very soon that his hopes were in vain.

CHAPTER ELEVEN

Sword to Ploughshare

'I have taken a heavy charge in arranging the business of the family'

DRUMCHARRY was, and is, set in a beautiful part of the Highlands. Alexander Irvine, when he had been minister of Fortingall in the first years of the nineteenth century wrote a description. 'From Duneaves the eye soon turns to Drumchary (the seat of Mr Stewart of Garth) when the beauties of Fortingall are seen to great advantage. It is adorned by lofty firs covering the ruin of an old circular fort or castle and by rows of planes and elms of a most majestic height. When the tempest rages, the noise of these trees is terrible beyond description, and rendered more so by the screams of the owl.

'Nature has beautifully varied Drumchary and art has not been idle. The lawns are edged with rows of laburnum, willow, ash and other trees in every variety. The banks varied with birch, fir and other forest trees, the streamlets concealed by their shade and the corn fields drawn to the scene, the ground divided, and the cattle grazing to favour the intentions of nature – the overhanging cliffs interspersed with trees, herbs, flowers, and the retiring heath rising on the mountains capped by the clouds presents a group of objects equally remote from the meanness and uniformity where the imagination is allowed to range and colours are admirably controlled, shade lengthening into shade and the sunbeam tinging the groves, dimpling in the streams, blazing in the cascades, or dazzling in the spangled rocks'.[100]

These were times of change in land ownership in the Highlands but, in spite of David's melancholia, society in his native straths was still much the same as it had been before the '45. A few nabobs with fortunes made in India or the Indies had bought estates but most of the lairds were members of the same families who had ruled the district for centuries. The road engineer, Joseph Mitchell, writing of the years when David ran the family estates, said: 'The Highlands of Perthshire presented at this time, 1825–8, a picture of great rural happiness ... almost all the lairds lived on their properties, engaged in improvements, took an interest in their tenants, and promoted by their influence the advancement of clever lads who were born on their estates ... To me, an outsider, looking back, this district at that time exhibited a very happy state of society. Each class was contented in its own sphere, and, as far as I could tell, there were few jealousies. The whole people were comfortable, and lived and moved among each other in a genial and kindly atmosphere'.[101]

The Duke of Atholl was the most powerful figure. The Earl of Breadalbane's lands were more extensive but ran west away from Atholl into Argyllshire from his seat at Taymouth where he had just completed an enormous new Gothic castle. In the summer of 1820, he entertained Prince Leopold who was widower of the King's only child, Princess Charlotte, and would later be elected king of the Belgians.

David attended and described the scene to Lord James Murray: 'Lord Breadalbane made a very fine display of his influence as a Highland Chieftain in honour of Prince Leopold on the 13th inst. With only a warning of 30 hours 1238 of his tenants, all men in the full vigour of life, fit for any service, and in full Highland dress, dined on the lawn in front of the Castle. As the spectators were very numerous, and all in their best clothes, and the women in tartan plaids and ribbons, the whole had a very imposing effect'.[102] Nothing, one feels, could have more impressed the colonel, but on the way home 'my gig overturned and gave me injuries to head, left shoulder and leg which have confined me to the house ever since'.

Sir Neil Menzies had lands on the north shore of Loch Rannoch as well as in Strathtay. Downriver began the estates of the Stewarts of Grantully and Murthly which marched against Atholl on the south bank of the Tay to well beyond Dunkeld. The

80-odd lairds who constituted the rest of local society were more modest.

The Glenlyon Campbells were still neighbours at Fortingall – *Fear Ghart* had looked after the legal business of most of the district while *An Doctair Mor*, Dr David Campbell of Glenlyon, looked after their health on an equally unpaid basis. The chief of the Clan Donnachaidh's successor was soon to rent a house half a mile and a minute's ferry ride across the Lyon from Drumcharry. His unpretentious lifestyle can be discerned from a neighbour's letter. 'We had a visit from Capt Robertson and all his family from Duneaves. They came to dinner on Monday and stayed all night on their way to Strathgarry. The Capt really makes a most patriarchal appearance trudging along beside his covered cart containing his wife, his three children, and his servants.' [103]

Fear Ghart, who had suffered a stroke 14 years earlier, was a beloved old character, still 'surrounded by his numerous and contented tenantry', offering lavish hospitality to anyone who passed. William had taken over management of the estates after his father's illness in 1806. The piping school in the farm sheds behind the mansion house had closed but there was still Duncan MacGregor. He and his twin sister were simple and had been raised in *Fear Ghart*'s kitchen which was seen as the obvious home for them when they proved too much for their mother, the young widow of a crofting tailor.

A tale survives from the childhood of these two. Robbie Uncle was a great favourite of theirs and he would come and spend part of the summer at Drumcharry. One evening, in 1804, the children became very excited, running to the front door saying that they had heard the old lawyer's carriage and he had come to visit even though he was not expected. The news came a day or two later. The old man died in Edinburgh at the moment the twins had rushed through from the kitchen.

In 1820 Duncan was a young man who wandered the district and even went as far as Edinburgh. Always clad in an ill-matched assortment of Highland garb of both sexes, he was known universally as Garth's Fool and he begged for his living as a truly appalling piper. When the colonel came home, he became Duncan's 'hero of heroes and earthly providence and deity'.[104]

David was the second son, with no expectation that he would inherit the property. William may have been the heir and a magistrate like his father but his younger brother had a national reputation and was much more worldly and sophisticated. Neither of the two had married, nor had John in the West Indies. The only heirs in the next generation were Jessie Irvine's offspring. Both William and his father considered the operation of the family estates their business and not David's. He would have agreed. He would have been proud that this patch of the Highlands still carried on the old way of life whose destruction elsewhere was causing him such concern, and would know that the welcome and respect shown to him by the country people were as much a tribute to the popularity of his father as to his own.

But after the dinner of the Celtic Society in July 1820, he wrote again to MacGregor-Murray. 'It was with a regret which I still find in full force that made me leave you so early the night of the Celtic meeting, the truth is, I never was in worse spirits or worse contented for a meeting of the Society, than that night'.[105] He went on to explain the cause with typical candour.

'My father who is not like you, as able for business as when thirty years of age, has for many years given up the whole charge of his affairs to my older brother, who unfortunately has no talent for business, indeed from natural causes is totally incapable, and the melancholy failure in my father's mind is too evident from the circumstances that for 14 years he never enquired how matters were managed, or what my brother was doing. I perceived much mismanagement in the farm of this place, and that two men did not do the work of one and the produce of 150 acres arable and good green pastures barely supplied the family, but believing that other matters went on well and that the mismanagement was confined to these parts I did not, from delicacy, enquire. My poor brother has one talent of which he has made too much use – that is the art of concealing his mismanagement, but in this he was supported by the unlimited confidence of the people ...

'My brother kept no books – not even a Rent roll – he received money from one man and paid it away to another without frequently even a memorandum and so incredibly negligent that Bills due my father amounting with interest which has not been called, for the last 13 years, to £4235 10s are allowed to run, and two of the holders very dishonourably claim prescription and refuse payment. No fortune could long withstand such management.

'Of all this I knew nothing and suspected nothing till, five days before the Celtic meeting, Dr Irvine informed me of a few particulars and on farther enquiry I discovered that an immediate interference was necessary – I could not think of being absent from the meeting and you in the chair – I staid there to the last moment – Early next morning I set off for Perth with my father's man of business, and a friend, and when we arrived here explained to my father what I heard, and the necessity of making my brother come to a full disclosure.

'This was done and I am sorry to say that he has incurred very many debts all borrowed in small sums from the country people ... without a vestige to show how the money has been expended – My father and brother (my brother enjoys an estate [Kynachan] by his mother of £650 a year) have executed a deed of trust for me to manage the whole.

'I beg, my good sir, that you will excuse my freedom in troubling you with this family detail, but I cannot rest satisfied in my mind till I explain the cause of my leaving you in the chair so early and my stupidity and low spirits during the evening – when I was informed that men threatened to arrest my brother's rents it was a cause for low spirits which I could not publickly explain. However I hope soon to put things to proper track'.

David had already been in discussion with Irvine about the problems. 'I have taken a heavy charge in arranging the business of the family – not but that I could get through with ease and expedition if I had the means, and if my father and brother would fully tell me their situation. William in particular is incredible and indeed my father equally so. The debts are great. I cannot at present command money to pay off one half. Will you send me a correct list of all debts in your parish and neighbourhood, and say who want their money immediately and who have not had their interest paid? I will send you a few hundred to pay off the most pressing.

'Bills to the amount of £3250 are due my father. Interest has never been paid on any of them – some with interest due for sixteen and eighteen years – others claim prescription as interest nor principal were never asked, and now refuse payment. There are claims of near £1000 against Mr Garden, all which he refuses, so there will be a lawsuit. Send me a correct list of all the debts you know – William will tell me nothing'.[106]

Father and brother took their feeble hands from the reins and allowed the energetic David to do as he pleased. In one way he must have seen this as an opportunity. He saw his neighbours beginning to clear tenants but this was anathema to him. Now he had a chance to demonstrate that improvements need not lead to removals. He could show that the existing tenants could be introduced to modern agriculture and produce better rents for the land owner than strangers.

But he also had the *Sketches* to see into production. The whole world knew that David Stewart, at the Duke of York's request, had been busy with the history of the Highland Regiments and that it would soon be published. Nor had the colonel made any secret about his intention to include a section critical of the way changes had been introduced into the Highlands and their effects on the people. Whilst he was still urgently addressing the problems caused by *Fear Ghart*'s debts and William's ineptitude, his brother-in-law mentioned rumours about the forthcoming book.

Stewart responded: 'My Annals of the Highland Regiments are by some supposed to favour the Radicals – Had I seen less of mankind and had I kept my eyes and ears shut to all that passes around me, I might be surprised at this supposition – but altho I am not surprised at this idea, I am not willing that such should be believed by those whose good opinion I value, and I regret to hear that an erroneous representation has been made to the Duke of

Athole of the intended publication, which instead of being republican, has been criticised for too much chivalry, too charged view of the state of society, and carrying the spirit of generous feeling, chivalry, and fidelity beyond its own bounds'.[107]

Being too busy sorting out his brother's affairs to visit the Duke and put his mind at rest, David sent Irvine a long outline of the book which 'as my writing is so difficult to be read, it will be made easy for His Grace if read by you'. The Duke was a close friend of Sir John Murray-McGregor and it is very likely that Sir John's thoughts on the draft of the manuscript of the *Sketches*, perhaps even its author's thoughts on the Duke's change of factors, had been communicated to His Grace.

'Now I am curious,' wrote Stewart, 'to hear what part of this work has been represented to the Duke of Athole as Democratic or Radicalistic – Is it in the feudal and patriarchal part? – the statistical, or the military essays? – no doubt it must be the views of the present state, in which I endeavour to show the policy of preserving a population so virtuous, economical and abstemious, the unpolicy of the harsh and unnecessary measures pursued in many cases ... and when I deprecate the burnings and depopulations of Lady Stafford, she would no doubt be happy to see the cry of Radicalism raised against me – but I care not for her opinion, nor wish to have any opinion or principle in common with a person who has caused such undeserved and general misery among so many thousands of virtuous unoffending human beings – But I have ever been most anxious for the Duke of Athole's good opinion which I am sure he will now give me when he knows the nature and scope of the work now ready for the Press ... I now send you ... part of the work which is <u>violent and radically</u> inclined, and if His Grace expresses a wish to see it, will you give it to him and when he has read it, will you favour me with his opinion – I need not again repeat how anxious I am for his good opinion ...'.

Irvine did what was asked of him and reported back to Drumcharry. The Duke thoroughly approved of what he heard and could not think where the idea of Radicalism had come from.

'This is quite what I anticipated,'[108] wrote Stewart. 'While I knew perfectly that His Grace would only smile at any idea of my entertaining radical notions I at the same time felt anxious that he should have a correct idea of my intended work – It was very natural for the Duke to suppose that with my warm feelings towards the Highlanders, I should be too ready to be led away by the clamour raised against Lady Stafford, and that I would allow myself to be imposed upon, and to receive as facts, the idle and perverted statements of interested people on a subject which has called forth such strong feelings, and so greatly attracted the attention of the public'.

But Stewart had not sent the most sensitive section of all. Now, having sweetened the Duke, he dared to. 'I will send a part of my MS which includes the most delicate and the most radical subject of the whole work – It is the most delicate because this, on the Sutherland estate, is the only part where names are mentioned – indeed the only part where the smallest allusion is made to persons ... Will you read the MS and then give it to the Duke, who I hope will favour me with his opinion, and I beg that you will at the same time add your own – I need not say with freedom and candour, as you know how anxious I am for correctness.

'I had some thoughts of omitting this part, but it is so connected with the whole of my subject – the chivalrous – the political economy, and the military, that this cannot be – besides, I am under the control of my Commanding officers the Booksellers – whom I have consulted on this part, and they wont permit a line to be omitted – however I am quite ready to correct and alter as may be pointed out'.

From the Duke, Irvine had borrowed and sent to Drumcharry the newly published book written by James Loch which justified the policy followed in Sutherland. The colonel was not impressed with it.

'I will read Mr Loch's book with attention and return it safe – I have not time to read it before I dispatch the MS – I have glanced over several pages, and see nothing but what I know before, and what I have seen in pamphlets and newspapers – the same eager anxiety to praise Lady Stafford and her generosity, and to run down the poor people. What are all the fine inns, fine farm steadings, fine farm houses, the mounds of earth to keep back the sea? What is all that to the poor tenants who have been so unmercifully ejected? I know the people – I know the country, and have information from honourable men who, I know, are incapable of deceiving me – Lady Stafford may mean well, and may be led away by specious plans – but I fear Mr Loch's book will not make me alter my opinion – that I wish to have no feeling in common with a person who, for the sake of gain, causes such misery to unoffending human beings'.

Patrick Sellar, the enforcer and later exploiter of Loch's clearing policy on the Sutherland estate, had been tried for culpable homicide following the death of an old lady. She had been manhandled from her cottage, forced to watch it burn, and died a few days later. The accused was acquitted but the obloquy stuck. Pamphleteers and the radical press had been sharply critical of the programme on Lady Stafford's lands in the north for some time but David Stewart was a member of the landowning gentry and, through his work with the Highland Society of London and his distinguished military career, had influence in London and throughout Scotland. His book was bound to be widely read and its opinions could not be lightly dismissed.

Dr Irvine brought this delicate passage of the book across the Tay by its new Telford-built bridge to Dunkeld House. The Duke had paid £42,000 for the bridge, and the toll he charged for the crossing caused considerable resentment. The extensive gardens and pleasure grounds of the Duke's southern seat were now laid out but the mansion house was still incomplete. It was not a good meeting.

'I am quite vexed,'[109] wrote David, 'for the trouble you have had with the MS and the time you lost in conversations with the Duke and Duchess regarding them. I was quite aware and expected that the Duke would not approve of the manner I treated the Sutherland improvements because it is in fact a virtual condemnation of part of his own measures, but I wish he had pointed out the most objectionable parts – The trouble is, I suppose, he objects to the whole ... I send you Mr Loch's book, which I hope you will send to Dunkeld House with my best acknowledgements for the reading of it – All that regards the Sutherland improvements I knew before – My objection to these improvements is that they are not for the good of the people – Of what benefit is it to the people of Athole that Rotmell has been improved with such elegance and outlay of money? Of what benefit is it to the Highlanders of Athole that Lude made great grazing farms on his estate, and that these farms send wool, mutton, and beef to market?

'I am anxious to see you about the farms of Litigan and Garth which are not yet settled – Were the Sutherland plan to be followed every old tenant on both estates would be ejected, and if not driven out of the country entirely, placed on two acres on the moor of Kynachan or some such spot to cultivate and improve, and left to live as they chose while great sums would be laid out in building houses for the rich tenants and on improvements on their farms.

'If my brother was to do all this to his honest old tenants, and place a Lothian farmer in the twelve merklands and a Tweeddale shepherd on the estate of Kynachan – then he would be a patriotic improver of his people, his country, and promote the prosperity of the State – Now I do believe, notwithstanding of Mr Loch's vindication of Lady S. that the tenants of the twelve merk land will be more respectable on their present farms even with the increase in rent than on her acres with State houses, whitewashed on the outside but little within'.

Raising two metaphorical fingers in the direction of His Grace the colonel sent off his manuscript to Constable in Edinburgh. After much correction it would be published two years later, but meantime his time was fully occupied in trying to set the estates on a sound footing.

CHAPTER TWELVE

Just and Honourable Arrangement

'I have a clear opinion myself of what I think ought to be done'

'STEWART FACED precisely the same dilemma as the landlords he so roundly and effectively condemned ... no man could have felt stronger sympathy for the people of the Highlands; they had no greater champion. Yet not even his great goodwill, nor the profits from the slave plantations ... was enough to place him above the necessity of shifting his people off their lands. The grip of the Highland problem was unyielding and sympathy was clearly not enough'.[110]

David Stewart's goodwill is not in question. The profits from the slave plantation are and these will be touched on in the next chapter, but did he clear his own lands in the quest for greater returns?

No neat run of estate papers has survived but enough information is available to give a reasonable idea of what his improvements were and their impact upon the tenantry. One imperfect source is the Rent Book of the family holdings from 1783 to 1820.[111] From it one can see that *Fear Ghart* had already considerably transformed the pattern of tenure on his estates by the time David took over their management. It would have been the old patriarch with his introduction of the potato in the 1770s who introduced the new crop rotations and swept away the old runrig system.

In 1784 the Rent Book names 60 tenants on separate farms. The numbers remained similar until 1802 when they began a steady decline. By 1807 there were 54 tenants, by 1811 44, the following year there were ten fewer and by 1818 there were 30. It is not as straightforward as it seems. Holdings disappear when they are amalgamated. Others spring into life, carved out of larger farms.

The largest imponderable is the keepers of the Rent Book. *Fear Ghart* kept it up until 1806 and then William took over. The father was notoriously indulgent to his tenantry and the son was notoriously incompetent. The wonder is that William kept the book at all during the latter years and its accuracy cannot be relied upon.

At the beginning of this period, the rents received from farming tenants amounted to £380. By 1817 they had risen to £430. The progression was not steady. 1810 produced more than £500. Some tenants paid no rent. Mungo Reid in Pitkerril on the Kynachan estate was one. He had eloped in 1768 with *Fear Ghart*'s young sister-in-law, Effie Stewart, and the farm was treated as part of her tocher. Other tenants would not have paid because they could not afford to and *Fear Ghart* was too soft-hearted to expel them. It would appear that, when rents were rising fast throughout the Highlands, on the Stewart estates they rose no more than 13% in half a century.

Recorded population figures for Fortingall – the parish included Rannoch and Glen Lyon – are 3,875 in 1801. In 1821, when David took over the management of the estates, they stood at 3,189. In 1831 when he had relinquished them, the total figure was 3,067. Serendipitously the census taker of 1841 was the school-master of Fortingall, Duncan Campbell. He was a local historian, later a journalist, and his *Book of Garth and Fortingall* is unlikely to be superseded as the standard work on the district.

In his census return, Campbell says that he has 'taken the liberty of giving comparative statements of the population' and goes on to say that 'the cause of the great and general decrease is the uniting of two or more farms into one by which the dispossessed are necessitated to seek employment & residence in other quarters'.

The figures are broken down into districts. District 1 consists of the estates of Garth, Drumcharry and Inchgarth. In 1821, when David was at the point of introducing his reforms, the population on his lands, excluding Kynachan, stood at 198 males and 236 females. In 1831, after he had completed them, there were still 197 resident males but the females had declined by 10.

The numbers seem to have remained virtually the same, but were some cleared to be replaced by more efficient outsiders? Again it appears that the colonel practised what he preached. The estates housed dynasties of tenants: Andersons, who had been MacGregors but changed when the name was proscribed, Stewarts, many descended from the Wolf of Badenoch like their laird, McDougalls, and Irvines. This last family has been examined in some detail.

For several generations the Irvines had been migrating west along Strathtay as tenants on various estates – prosperous tenants, for they could set up their sons on farms of their own. The first in Fortingall was James, born in 1732, who was a tenant on Inchgarth when he married in 1761 and later held the Garth farms of Over Blairish and Ringam. Each of his sons married girls who lived on *Fear Ghart*'s land. John was the eldest. He had a holding of his own on Garth by 1793 and was still alive on the same farm in 1841 aged 79, living with his 75-year-old sister and looked after by his middle-aged spinster daughter. Farming next door was the youngest of his seven children, John, and his family.

The second of James's sons was Duncan. He succeeded his father in the tenancy of the little farm of Ringam, high on the brae face above Garth Castle. Duncan married a girl 20 years younger than himself and had 12 children. One, James, was a prosperous tenant on Litigan, a little down the hill from Ringam, in 1841. His old father had a household on the same farm with a 20-year old daughter and 15-year-old son still at home.

The third of this patriarch's sons was Neil and he is found going into partnership with John Anderson when a couple of farms were amalgamated in 1821. The fourth son was Alexander. He became a minister and eloped with *Fear Ghart*'s youngest daughter. The same sort of story can be told of several of these families. All had been settled on *Fear Ghart*'s estates when David took over, and all were still there when David's management ceased.

The colonel explained the policy he intended to follow to his brother-in-law. 'The capital of a bare soil and precarious climate is the manual labour of a hardy, economical, abstemious race of men – My brother has destroyed some of this capital by going on the theory that any man who labours hard ought to have as much as two horses can work and manage'.[112]

This regime meant that much of the land was not being fully utilised. Two horses required a gang of hired men, and if the tenant did not have the money or the inclination to exploit his plot he left it derelict. 'This is a very plausible theory but the practice would ruin many an industrious moral family in the Highlands and lessen the rent to the landlord. Two horses are fully sufficient to labour the farm of Garth. I think it more advantageous to the country and the landlord that it should be occupied by those tenants whose personal labour with that of their children would improve and meliorate the soil, rise the produce, and carry on all work at less expense than can be done by hired servants or day labourers, consequently the people will be more independent and be able to pay a better rent. The soil in the Highlands should be improved by the labours of the occupier fed and clothed and supported in all necessary expenses by the produce'.

This was the antithesis of the doctrine of the agricultural improvers. They wished to remove the small occupiers and replace them with large tenants who could practice economies of scale. Stewart wanted to encourage more efficient subsistence farming. This could well yield more than amalgamated units but the families of the small farmers would consume the output themselves. On the one hand, the produce of the land could be exported to feed town dwellers. On the other it would feed greater numbers of the indigenous inhabitants.

The colonel was still making such ringing declarations of policy when considering the detail of his changes. 'As I intend to propose a new arrangement of my father's land (but no change of tenant except Duncan McDiarmid and Duncan McGregor and McDougall if they have no lease and will not give more rent) I will be much obliged for your ideas on the subject as you mention in your last letter – My object is to make a just and honourable arrangement equally conducive to the welfare of the landlord and the tenant and I will be most grateful for any information and assistance – I have a clear opinion myself of what I think ought to be done – but my opinion is equally clear that I may form a wrong opinion'.

The minister had pulled himself up to the ranks of the gentry thanks to his profession and his unorthodox marriage to the laird's daughter. Much as he appreciated his position as confidant of his distinguished brother-in-law, he still had three elder brothers who were tenants on the hill overlooking Strathtay and his advice would have been carefully phrased.

The colonel responded with his thanks. 'I am much obliged by your letter on the arranging of lands. Time will not admit of my answering it at present – indeed it will be better to discuss the whole when we meet. Nothing can be better than the abstract part of your letter, but it is by a few facts and by taking examples from what is passing around that we must be guided, after a good foundation is laid in sound honourable principles'.[113]

This was not uppermost in David Stewart's mind, however. He had discovered the family faced disaster. 'I tell you now in confidence, and beg that it will be kept in confidence and not to be hinted, for it will be known all too soon. The interest on the debts I have already discovered exceeds the present rental of the three estates including this farm, by £390 a year. In short, that sum must be borrowed to pay the interest, and every ounce of victuals consumed in this house must be on borrowed money, so that if the rents of this place and Garth do not exceed £700 – and if Kynachan will not bring £21 or £22 thousand pounds, Garth must also be sold.

'You will observe this is only calculating on the debts I know, for my father and brother will tell me nothing – indeed William's object seems to be to conceal all he can, and it is only by sending out persons to enquire among the country that I can discover bills – I have discovered too much – I have discovered £26,375 of debts and the rents are not at this moment £1000 – even if they were all paid which is not the case. So you see the task I have undertaken and this too with such men whose object seems to be to conceal all that they have been doing. The family must leave, and I purpose putting this house and place in order [and] hope it may be let as a shooting quarter. I know not where my father and brother can be placed or where a cheap place can be found – it is impossible they can remain here – the subject altogether is most distressing'.

It was not just that the land must surely be sold after several centuries of occupation by the family, but honour was at stake. The colonel explained the Highland attitude to financial failure in the *Sketches*: 'Insolvency was considered disgraceful and *prima facie* a crime'.[114] He went on to describe how those who had lost their money used to be treated: 'Bankrupts were forced to surrender their all, and were clad in a party-coloured clouted garment, with the hose of different setts, and had their hips dashed against a stone in presence of the people, by four men, each taking hold of an arm or a leg, This punishment was called the *Toncruaidh*'.

There were small rays of hope, the best being brother John in the West Indies, or perhaps the colonel could still obtain an appointment from the government, or his book could prove a sensational success.

CHAPTER THIRTEEN

Spurious Relations

'Why dont you marry and preserve the family?'

JOHN STEWART, *Fear Ghart*'s youngest son, had moved from St Vincent to Grenada, and thence to Trinidad in 1808 when David was commanding the garrison. The relationship between the two brothers was cool. It was hoped that John would make his fortune and invest some of his wealth in developing the estates back home but it appeared that the opposite tended to be the case. John's war service culminated in his becoming a lieutenant in St John's Regiment of Militia on Grenada, and he possessed sufficient of the family charm to be presented with a gold medal in 1816 by the non-commissioned officers and privates of his company as a 'token of esteem and attachment'.[115]

The planter was kept informed about the dire nature of the family finances. He was looked on by David as the best hope of salvation, as well as being profoundly irritating. John owned Garth Estate, the only family holding in the West Indies. It lay east of San Fernando, where he had a warehouse, in the heart of the sugar-growing area towards the south of the Island. David had lent money to set this up and continued to put capital into it in the hope of returns to alleviate the problems back home but John was both indolent and inefficient.

'I had a long letter from John yesterday,'[116] wrote the colonel to Irvine in July 1821, 'he is well and doing well, but is now of a stand for want of money – He is now doing that which he ought to have done nineteen years ago and if even a couple of thousand pounds could be sent to him, it would set him completely on his legs – Had he followed the plan I recommended to him twenty two years ago, and I came from the Mediterranean on purpose to set it agoing, and had got money ready to send him, he would now be what others are, who did what he ought to have done — that is, with an income of five or six thousand a year — Ask at Mr John Bisset what is the income of Rob Sutherland, J. Cumming, Gilbert Munro, Willm Menzies, and others of St Vincent — John had better opportunities than they had — However his eyes are now opened and if he has health it may not yet be too late'.

John had built a curing house, a boiling house, a magass house, and a mill — cattle-driven, rather than the most up-to-date steam. He had 31 slaves labouring on his sugar, a modest number when some Scots planters had over 500 and demand for the commodity had not slackened since the war.

But money from the West Indies to support the Perthshire estates did not materialise. In 1827 David's eldest nephew, Sandy Irvine, wrote on his uncle's behalf to John. The colonel 'observed that he has remitted since he had charge of his father's and brother's affairs 4 or £5000, I forget which, under the confident expectation of regular remittances to reimburse him ... Of this sum he has only received £500 which was some years ago and nothing since'.[117]

The capital was handed over in 1823, the year John returned to Scotland for a few months — and had his portrait painted by Sir Henry Raeburn in the closing days of the artist's life. David's security for the money was one third of the Caribbean plantation. The younger brother also came home with one of his bastards. The planter had lived with Charlotte Tobin whom he had met on Grenada and she had recently died. They had a daughter Ann on whose birth certificate Charlotte is described as a 'free coloured Woman'. The Tobins were an old French planter family on the island and leading apologists and promoters of slavery. Charlotte may have been a source of embarrassment to them, certainly more so than Ann's existence was to John. Having natural children was so common amongst planters, especially those who were unmarried, as to be almost the rule.

John fathered another five recorded offspring from at least three women who were quite likely to have been his slaves. There are indications that three of these children who were boys were set up in apprenticeships after their father's death in 1832. It may well be that John felt that without her mother the 13-year-old Ann would not easily fit into his menage. So he brought her to Scotland and left her at Drumcharry.

Clementina was delighted by the arrival of her niece. As the colonel told Irvine, Jessie needed to be won over. 'I am sorry that my sisters do not feel as I do with regard to the propriety and delicacy of introducing the spurious product of so indiscreet and ill-timed a connexion, as one of the family,' [116] he wrote, using 'spurious' in its original meaning of illegitimate. 'I must except Jessie who, I believe, feels as I do and that she only yields to her sister'.

How Ann coped with life as a coloured girl in early nineteenth century rural Perthshire is a mystery. After 1824 there is but a single reference to her – in a letter to Jessie in the 1850s – when she is revealed as unmarried, acting as her aunt's companion and living with her in Pitlochry in Craigatin, the house of her aunt's second son William Irvine the local doctor. In the 1851 Census she is described as the doctor's cousin. She died in 1859 after a stroke; William Irvine filled in her death certificate, again giving his relationship to her as 'cousin'. She is buried in Moulin churchyard in her own separate grave beside those of other members of the family, but her relationship is not obscured by the inscription which says that she died at Craigatin.

A neighbour, the wife of Captain Duncan Robertson of Kindrochet, commented on the planter's arrival in a letter to her husband, then in Ireland with his regiment: 'John Stewart Garth has come home in bad health, poor man (in consequence, they say, of his disappointment at losing the fair Elenora – the effects of a bad climate is more likely cause however) he means to go out again as soon as he is able – he has brought home one of his Black pets to leave with his sister'.[119] Depositing one's Black or even Brown pets on Scottish relations was quite common. A similar connection was wished upon the Stewarts of Ardvorlich, 20 miles to the south, and on the earls of Mansfield.

Ann became part of Jessie Irvine's family at the manse in Birnam. Her six cousins, the minister's children, ranged from young Alexander (Sandy) who was in his late teens and following in his father's footsteps by studying for the ministry at St Andrews, down to sickly James John aged 8.

A bill from the Dunkeld haberdasher survives which shows Ann being outfitted. When she first arrived she would have been wearing mourning for her mother, and, as it happened, another death in the family soon occurred. In 1825 she is re-clothed – shoes, wrist cuffs, muslin gloves and a variety of materials including satin, 'Brown Tweed bombazette', cotton, flannel, foundation muslin, calico, as well as thimbles, and hooks and eyes to sew them into garments. She had a season ticket to walk across Telford's toll bridge over the Tay each day on her way to school, but she seems to have attended classes for no more than six weeks.[120]

David was surely too intelligent to miss the irony of the contrast between his position on slavery and his indignation at the treatment of Highlanders. He describes the slave trade in his book as 'that atrocious and inhuman traffic',[121] but this was years after all the European powers had declared it illegal. He had given information to James Stephen on the Abolition Committee but at the same time had ensured he maintained the goodwill of the West Indian slave owners. He also invested in and hoped to profit from his brother's plantation.

He never married. In 1821 he wrote rather bitterly on the subject to Irvine. 'Whether I am in Edinburgh or in Perth – whether in Dunkeld or in Athole – I am assailed and teased with the same cry – Why dont you marry and preserve the family? – From Inver to Lochlyon – from Logierait to Dunan, or Dalnacardoch, if I step into a house whether gentry or tenantry, it is the same – if I speak to an acquaintance on the road, who is intimate with the family, nine times out of ten – in short high and low it is the same cry – your elder brother will never marry – the younger is in the W Indies, why don't you marry and prevent the entrance of strangers in to a family which the whole country is anxious to preserve? – thus I am constantly teased – my only answer is silence as I can't afford to marry'.[122]

He may not have been able to afford to marry but he was not sexually inactive. Fathering illegitimate children was a regular and unremarkable pastime for the local gentry. David had uncles and great uncles who left bequests to children born out of wedlock. Six years after his wife's death *Fear Ghart* had an illegitimate son, Alexander, born of Elizabeth McGregor from Tynadalloch on Drumcharry in 1789.

When home on leave, particularly in the year after Maida, David would have got to know the lad. He was reared by his mother and his father bought him a commission. He resigned when a captain in the 94th Regiment on marrying the daughter of a non-commissioned officer. He went to Canada and took as his second wife the daughter of a baronet. David had tried to help him in a letter of 1818 to Colonel Dick of the 42nd. 'I am not sure if you know that I have a brother a lieut and adj to the late 95th *(sic)*. He is now like many others on half pay and likely to remain so for life unless some exertion is made'.[123] Elizabeth, this Alexander's mother, may well have had an equally obliging younger sister for Mary McGregor in the same township gave William Stewart at least one recorded moment of passion when he sired her daughter, born in 1795.

In her memoirs, written at the height of Victorian prudery, Elizabeth Grant of Rothiemurchus reminisces about the year 1813. She tells of their respectable cook who bore one such child by the married manager of the estate forests. This man and his wife regularly dined at the laird's table. 'There was no attempt to excuse, much less conceal her history; in fact, such occurrences were too common to be commented upon ... It was a curious state of manners; I have thought of it often since'.[124]

David Stewart had at least two children about this time and one can suppose that his genes as well as those of his brother are scattered across the Caribbean. In the Fortingall register is an entry: 'Jean, natural daur to Col. David Stewart of Garth & Christian McLean in Drumcharry, 23rd December 1823'.

Christian McLean was 27, the daughter of a tenant. In 1835 when there was a great pay-out to creditors of the estates she was living at Balnacraig on Drumcharry, was owed £131–3–8d, and was asking for a further £200.[125] In 1841 she was still on the estate, a 45-year-old spinster in a cottage of her own which she shared with her 18-year-old daughter.

Stewart had one other child, a son, about this time whose birth date is not known. Unlike Jean it seems that Neil's mother must have died at or soon after he was born since, along with Ann, he became the responsibility of his long-suffering aunt Jessie in 1823. He moved in with her eldest son Sandy in 1830 who took care of his young cousin's education. Afterwards, wrote Sandy Irvine, 'he wished to go to the West Indies. From this, considering the state of West Indian affairs, I thought to dissuade him, and he then fixed on being a sailor. Accordingly I got him apprenticed on board a merchant ship in the West India trade, which he can leave and adopt the profession of a planter, should such a step appear hereafter to be advisable'.[126]

Poor Neil was a disappointment. He pops up in a letter of 1837 to Sandy Irvine from his younger brother David. 'Neil is a gentleman's servant in Edinburgh. Confound his craven spirit – he might have been master of a ship and a gentleman'. Six months later there is news of him from Edinburgh. 'I called at Robert Stewart's the day I received your letter but found that he & Neil had gone off to Perth that morning to try and recover a bag of clothes which Neil had lost about the coach offices the last time he was in Perth. On Monday last the Major returned my call when he told me that he left Neil at Perth where he is to remain till Tuesday when he expected to get over here on some of the coaches being from weakness unable to travel on foot as his companion had done.

'I called again on Tues & Wed & this morning but the Stewarts have heard nothing of or concerning Neil since Monday. The Major told me that they did not get the clothes of which poor Neil stands very much in need, but they got a promise of some little money as a compensation.

'Neil's health is recovering fast and his mind is almost perfectly restored. Stewart thinks that if he had some little money to get clothes and was properly fed for a week or ten days that he might go in to any situation. Stewart, who by the way is the most complacent and self-satisfied little man I have met with in an age, thinks that Neil is of a wayward and unsteady turn of mind and the last illness will render him more so than ever'.[126]

This is the last that is heard of him.

CHAPTER FOURTEEN

Changes on the Estates

'I do not understand what dung is meant'

DAVID STEWART prided himself on being both rational and judicious and on applying these skills to sort out the frequently irrational behaviour of his fellow men. One senses a certain impatience in his dealings with those he considered less cool-headed than himself. He could never have made such a mess of the family finances as his father and William and he could never have left so gifted an administrator as himself unemployed when the West Indian colonies were crying out for leadership.

But the re-organisation of the estates was now his first priority and he gave the problem the full benefit of his attention. As he wrote to Irvine in 1820. 'I generally feel more satisfied with myself and better in every way when my time is fully occupied, as I find idleness a fatiguing tiresome concern. I seldom want employment'.[127]

William was sent off to Auch, a large sheep property to the west beyond Tyndrum, which was occupied by a remote cousin. He complains rather miserably about the condition of his eyesight before dying there the following year. *Fear Ghart* was to have joined his eldest son but he seems to have been too decrepit to make the journey in what were clearly the last months of his life.

David was a soldier. He had taken an interest in the operations of sugar plantations in the West Indies but, although he had decided views on how estates in the Highlands should be run, he was in the army when still a boy and his practical knowledge of agricultural management was weak. He relied on Alexander Irvine for advice.

'I wish to draw up a few regulations for the tenants,' he wrote, 'and if Mr Graham [the Duke's factor] will give me a copy of their regulations, I would be much obliged – I only want a few plain regulations easily understood and easily followed'.[128] He goes on to tell of changes already taking place amongst the tenants. 'David McLeish in Balnarn has resigned. William Stewart goes to his farm. John Dewar and James McBean go to America, and this will enable us to put Tombreck in two divisions instead of four. There are many offerers – probably Neil Stewart the Miller will get the half for his second son. James Dewar who never paid more than fifty shillings for the half of Pitkerril (the other paid the rest of the rent) goes to America, John Stewart his neighbour gets the whole farm leaving two small crofts'.

He then proceeds to give his views on emigration, one of the critical issues of the time and the subject of Alexander Irvine's book nearly 20 years earlier. 'As to emigration, I have wished to encourage voluntary Emigration, and that thinning of the population which is absolutely necessary – but I am decidedly hostile to the desolating system of turning out and extirpating a whole race – but without emigration, as the Lowlands, how can a man in this country provide for four or five sons when he has so many? It is not every tenant that left four sons in farms as Euan McDougall in Balnacraig has done – nor is it often that three brothers are as close as your brothers are. Without emigration from Fortingall they could not have got their farms – but the Emigrations which made room for them were voluntary'.

In another letter from this period Stewart talks about a new tenant on Kynachan, probably the minister's nephew, the son of his brother John. 'Your namesake gets Kynachan, rent £130 but if he improves, clears the ditches, encloses and cultivates new land to the amount of £90 every year for a few years, he will be allowed the third of this outlay – the work to be examined and valued twice a year by two experienced men. The rent must be paid in the first instance – if he works he gets back £30 – if he does not work he will get nothing.

'This rule I propose to follow with all the tenants – and as there is much good land to bring into cultivation, and a sufficient number of able active and willing men, I hope a few years will add a third to the present arable, and enclose the whole – the expense will be heavy in the first instance – but it is only temporary, and the high rents the improvements will enable them to pay will be permanent and no doubt will increase. The tenants ask no lease – I only promise they will not be removed while they conduct themselves properly, and that their rents will not be rised for a certain period – when the tenants place such confidence in me I must shew that I deserve it'.[127]

It was a remarkable act of trust in their new laird that the tenants did not want leases. In the *Statistical Account* of 1791–9, the minister of Dull, whose parish contained Kynachan, said this of the people: 'Their condition, however, might be meliorated if proprietors would grant them leases of their farms. All of them are tenants that may be removed at the proprietors will. It has been said, that they would become independent if leases were granted to them; but experience shews that this objection is ill-founded'. It might be worth remembering that *Fear Ghart* would die owing the equivalent of some four years' rent to his tenants, which surely gave them a sense of security.

The colonel was involved in the minutiae. 'You mention in your last letter about dung and going to law on the subject. I do not understand what dung is meant or what is the subject, but surely there is no cause for speaking about going to law – you will explain the whole when we meet. Patullo says he never had any dispute with the tenants – on the contrary he is on the best terms – he sent John Anderson to me last week to tell me to put the tenants on their guard, as the new supervisor would perhaps soon go round – the warning had a good effect for when he came round he found only a few pecks of malt in Overblairish'.[129]

Patullo was the obliging excise officer at Kenmore. In 1823 there were 14,000 prosecutions for illegally distilling whisky in Scotland.[130] The following year the landowner was made liable for stills found on his land, which dealt the industry, which was one of the few generators of cash in the Highlands, a severe blow.

One discordant note has survived. The sub factor at Blair, James

Findlater, wrote a letter to his superior, Frederick Graham, in July 1824, a few years after David's takeover, which passed on a piece of gossip. Graham was the man to whose appointment in place of the 'judicious and honourable' Captain Stewart David so strongly objected in 1820. 'Col David Stewart of Garth after his song of praise upon his selected few for their continued consideration to their highland tenantry now begins to play up the other tune. On the estate of Kynachan he is said to have warned his tenantry there (who have no leases) to pay additional Rents or remove at the first term. Among others Donald Stewart in Tummel Bridge Inn has got the general intimation that his possession now £50 must be £80 rent from Whitsunday next. Donald says that the Colonel's word of honour upon which his possession depends is not much better than a common Highlanders, for he had it so often repeated that no offer of a higher rent or other inducement should ever affect him that Donald declares he is no man at all, that could say so much and act so contrary'.[131]

In 1820 the Kynachan estate was to be exposed on the open market to satisfy creditors but the sharp drop in sheep prices made it unlikely that a satisfactory offer would be received. The neighbouring lairds, Sir Niel Menzies and John Stewart of Foss, were busy talking the price down from the £13,000 that David hoped for to something nearer £11,000. Meantime he was busy trenching the rough grazing, turning the soil to an unheard-of nine-inch depth and having the stones removed.

He was also planting trees. 'I would wish to plant with a few ornamental trees of the largest sized plants, such as spruce firs, maple, limes, planes etc. Have any of your nurseries any plant of six or less years growth? What do they charge for 1000 spruce for plants of two years old, and 1000 of the same age of beech, lime, elms, planes, horn beam?'[132] Just south of Craig Kynachan 'I am happy to find that the Daldu plantation promises well – The soil is beyond all expectations, the stones seem as if they had been laid on the top, as six inches under they are extremely numerous, but under the strata which is so close with round small stones that they seem as if they laid down on purpose, the soil is deep and perfectly clear of stones ... As the expense of seedling plants is moderate and having the ground prepared and good for the purpose, it cannot be more profitably employed than as a nursery.

'Will you have the goodness to direct Mr Christie to send by Buchanan an additional quantity of 5000 Larch, 3000 Oak, 300 Norway spruce, 300 Ash, 500 Beech, 300 Elm, 3000 Scotch Fir, 300 Plane, 300 Willow. These will help to fill up the prepared ground, and whatever becomes of this place, the trees will be valuable either in the nursery or if planted'.

There are passing references to crofts being carved out of other holdings or being snuffed out, the land being distributed amongst their neighbours, and of often unsuccessful attempts to cajole a tenant from one farm to another, and of tenants letting him down. Neil Stewart, the miller on Kynachan, wanted and was offered half the farm of Tombreck for his son, but 'behaved ill'.

The best documented of the changes to the pattern of landholding of the tenants refers to Litigan. This farm lies on the hillside above Garth Castle. Now it is grassland and forestry plantation but on the high slopes the traces of the intricate field system still remain and there are two lines of head dykes, one a hundred or so yards higher up the hill than the other. It is tempting to identify this extension to the useful land as being from the time of the colonel's improvements.

Litigan was split into six tenancies – three on east Litigan and three on west. When it was measured in 1791, the surveyor found about 20 acres of infield and 20 of outfield on each farm which was subdivided amongst the six tenants.

In 1821 it was decided to make west and east Litigan over to single tenants. John Anderson was to be tenant of the west and Duncan Irvine, second of the minister's three siblings, to take the east. Duncan Irvine whinged about the division to his younger brother who passed on his misgivings to the colonel. The latter wrote back: 'I observe what you say about Duncan Irvine in consequence of his communication with you. Twelve months ago this communication would have surprised me, but the experience

I have had of character, line of conduct, and principles of some of our tenants has given me new ideas, and new views, very unexpected on my part, and will learn me to hold a very different opinion of them than I formerly held'.[133]

David had written his book in which the Highlander was depicted as being almost saintly in the quantity of noble virtues with which he was endowed. It seems to have been a rude shock to discover that he was also loaded with the usual peasant vices. Accompanied by the two tenants and witnesses the laird himself had puffed up the hill, marking the boundaries between the farms with stones, doing his best to accommodate the wishes of both parties. The arguments had lengthened the task and it continued the next day under Charles McDiarmid, a cousin and the young laird of Bohally, who was studying medicine.

'Charles was there two days, and so completely complied with my directions to attend to the wishes and suggestions of the Tenants that to please D Irvine and meet his wishes, the marches were altered three times – D Irvine said that the next outfield was unlucky – that no man's cattle lived there, and that he wished not to have it – McDiarmid explained that it was the best share, but he still persisted, from his dread of this unlucky field which killed cattle – The third day Chas McDiarmid after long discussion settled the Division – when all was finished John Anderson told D Irvine – Now, says he, if you prefer my lot I am ready to exchange with you (only that I retain my house on which I have taken so much pains) as if you please, and if Col S allows it, will you make a division of your own, and I will draw lots which of the lots made by you will come to my share – D Irvine answered that he was quite satisfied.

'Now this is the man who was present two and three days when so much pains was taken to please him (not upon his account, but that of my sister and yours) when my line was drawn before his face, himself frequently, if not always, fixing the landmarks and stones on the marches – this is the man who told you on a Sabbath day after hearing the Word of God – that the marches were not pointed out to him'.

Duncan Irvine waited until the laird had gone down to London in the autumn before having another go at his younger brother. The minister wrote to Stewart to report that old *Fear Ghart* was dying – his death took place in November – and passed on the complaint.

David had been once again troubled by his old wound: 'the arm has suppurated, a vast discharge of foul matter has followed – the pain is gone, and I now only require my old remedies, time, care, and patience to be well again'.[134] His response to Duncan Irvine's griping was brusque: He 'was offered his choice – either the east side or the west side, as now divided, only that John Anderson was to keep his own steading. He preferred the east side – He will not be allowed to change – he must take the east side as it is or none unless indeed that J Anderson will again repeat his offer of an exchange – but I will not ask Anderson to do it – he made the offer and it was refused in my presence'.

The old laird died but the matter of Litigan was still not settled. The minister was dragged up to the farm, listened to his brother's complaints, had a quarrel with Charles McDiarmid and, after reporting *Fear Ghart*'s death and wishing his brother-in-law a return to good health, penned an uncharacteristically intemperate passage in a letter to David in London.

'... Before I stirred a foot I was easily satisfied as to Charles's inaccuracy & stupidity. I went east and surveyed the ground and found that Charles was wrong in every fact that D Irvine got no equivalent for what was taken off but the pen behind his barn yard for a wing of this ground below. All this on my return I reported to Charles in presence of his uncle D McDiarmid & told him my opinion of his skill and justice. Says he, take you one man and he'll take another & see how the farm was divided. With you I said I shall have nothing to do. I cannot comprehend how such glaring inequality should have been attempted against a poor man'.[135]

Another of the Irvine brothers, Neil, was also in bad odour with the laird. Alexander went on to say: 'Your antipathy now in public to these poor men who have been long faithful servants and tenants to your father is to me inexplicable. I cannot believe that their relation to me should be any objection – partiality on this account I did not expect or ask, but I expected preference on equal terms'. He seems to have finished with some bitter allusion to the legacy of his elopement those years ago with the colonel's sister. The response from his brother-in-law must have lifted his heart. David always began his letters to Irvine with 'Dear Sir'. On this and only this occasion, he varied the formula. 'Many and kind thanks, my Dear friend, for your offer of assistance in my renewed attack from my old tormentor ...'.

He goes on to write of his sister's marriage to Irvine. 'No persons have ever spoken or even hinted to me on the subject, but with an expression of regret and surprise – I strongly felt the same myself, and when I looked to my grandaunts, aunt, and sister I began to fear that elopements were to be hereditary in the family – but whatever my feelings were when I first heard (and I never had the least hint previously as I always discouraged tale bearers) of the marriage and its manner – my affection for my sister, my personal friendship for you, my respect for your talents and character, made me soon forget every feeling but that of a desire to promote your joint happiness and welfare – but a more universal feeling of disapprobation of your marriage and the manner it was conducted I have seldom seen ...

'My father was an honourable, kind-hearted man with as few faults as most men – he was fierce in his temper (from want of proper checks, not being in a society who would not bear his violence) – open to flattery – if he was called a kind master to tenants and saw his table full, and he was called hospitable, he looked not to the consequences for his family – these were his faults – he was a gentleman in mind, manner and appearance – he was just, honourable, and humane, he was a man of talents for public business – in a word he was such as his district will not soon see his equal – therefore let his fierce opposition to your marriage be forgotten, and as I know that you make every allowance for the frailty of his temper I hope I will hear no more allusions to the subject.

'Altho you have mentioned and hinted at it in many letters to me, this is the first time I have ever noticed the subject either by words as by the pen – It is the last and I particularly request that you will not answer or say a word on the subject – my father is dead. Long, long before he died all unpleasant feelings towards you and his daughter were forgotten – With the exception of one month after I heard of the marriage (I did then feel strongly) my feelings have ever been those of the truest affection, friendship, and the most anxious desire to promote the honour, happiness and prosperity of you and my sister and of your family.

'I again repeat my desire that you will not write a word on this subject – I have fully told you my sentiments – I know and feel that you are friendly towards me – my sentiments are unchanging and true – so are yours – therefore more need not be said – It will do no good and thus I have first noticed the subject – and thus have I finished it for ever'.[134]

Duncan Irvine never did take over East Litigan. His half was leased to John Menzies and James McDonald who may well have been sons of Alex Menzies and Neil McDonald who had been tenants there since 1795.

The results of David's improvements were noticed by the neighbours. After his first harvest, Sophia Robertson of Kindrochet wrote to her husband, in Ireland with his regiment.: 'Col David Stewart called here yesterday on his way from Athole House ... he has become the most successful farmer in all these countrys, Miss Flemming not excepted, for even this season while other peoples crops are scarcely worth cutting, his is as heavy as can grow – this is no rhodomontard for the crop has been sold at an enormous price'.[136]

Alas, his very success brought more debts forward. 'People say that they were unwilling to give additional trouble last year, when they saw so many claims,' David wrote, 'and kept back, but while the forbearance was commendable as it proceeded from such kindly motives, these unexpected demands are a cruel check upon me, and will overturn all my plans and expectations'.[137]

A week later David gave further details of his position. 'No more bills have appeared for three days so that I hope we have got the whole. The debts, old outstanding accounts, back interest, and the deficiency of the present Rents in comparison with the Interest of debts have swelled the gross amount to £7,000 beyond my estimate of past Martinmas. There are £3500 of back interest alone – so that unless the two estates sell for a price which I do not expect, Drumcharry must follow, and we may bid farewell to this country. I was in hopes that I could have got an appointment which would have given me an income from which I could spare sufficient to avert the blow, but I see no prospect'.[138]

Through his mother, Kynachan, itself mortgaged for £4,000, belonged to William outright. Garth, Drumcharry and Inchgarth, worth £20,000, carried debts of £38,000 – perhaps £2,000,000 today. However, David's book was about to be published and at least this should have taken his mind off his problems.

CHAPTER FIFTEEN

The Sketches

'One of the most interesting books that has fallen under our notice for a long period'

Concurrent with the colonel's efforts to sort out the family finances, he was preparing his manuscript for publication. Archibald Constable, his publisher, wrote in November 1820 saying that he had heard that still further changes to the manuscript were being contemplated. He recommended that 'you go ahead with the work without further delay'.[139]

Proofs arrived at Drumcharry the following month and Stewart fired back his opinion. Constable was unimpressed. He disagreed with David's preferred style of printing and said that, if it were adopted, the work would not sell, and Constable would not publish it. He went on to say that the print size of the footnotes had to be so tiny that corrections were 'perfectly intolerable'.[140] Unless alterations ceased, he would not print.

The threat silenced the author for some months, but the following August Constable was forced to respond again. No, the colonel could not add to Volume 1. It was too long already. Could he cut out the chapters about the Fencible Regiments?[141]

Stewart eventually settled on calling the book *Sketches of the Character, Manners, and Present State of the Highlanders of Scotland, with Details of the Military Service of the Highland Regiments*. He went down to Edinburgh to oversee the final touches. James Robertson, the young lawyer and diarist, paid him a visit in his lodgings. 'Col Stewart Garth's book is to be published some of these days. I saw him a few days ago. He was confined with the wound in his arm for some time but is now again recovered. I am the organ of communication between him and Mr Young at present. They are both zealous antiquaries, and of course antiquities form the subject of these communications, although I am rather fond of the study I now wish with all my heart these dry as dust descriptions were at an end.'[142]

Published in March 1822, the popularity of the Sketches was immediate. Nothing like it had ever been placed before the public. Books on the Highlands to date amounted to travellers' tales and romances. People like Dr Johnson, Boswell, and Pennant had all published details of their intrepid voyaging. James McPherson, with *Ossian*, and Walter Scott had added colour. The writings of the latter and the gallantry of the Highland soldiers during the wars had led to a resurgence of interest in their culture, and its romanticised aspects were fashionable. But the reality of Gaeldom, cut off from the rest of Britain by geography, language, and history, was little known. The press had written about the Sutherland Clearances but to those south of the Highland Line Dr Johnson's adage still largely held good. 'To the Southern inhabitants of Scotland, the state of the mountains and the islands is equally unknown with that of Borneo and Sumatra; of both they have heard little and guess the rest'.[143]

David did not pretend to be impartial. He was a Highlander himself and had all his ancestors' pride of race. He had commanded Highland soldiers and he knew they had been without equal in any army in the world. Nevertheless he tackled his task in his customary style by investigating the facts and building his picture with a host of tiny illustrative details. Now, of course, he is a great authority, his is the source book for countless works on the history and the customs of the Highlands but then his material was fresh; he was writing sociology as much as history and his methods and research still make it very good sociology, even if the history could now be thought a little weak.

Above all he was readable. Throughout his life, uninhibited fluency with the pen is a striking characteristic. He dashes off letters at high speed, pouring out his views almost as soon as they enter his head and often has an afterthought or two following his signature. He is always direct; he seems not to censor his thoughts and opinions nor have any doubts about them. His style is forthright and uses no literary tricks or fancies. He may have been sometimes verbose by modern standards but he is not dull. In an age when Walter Scott was a best seller, to his readers Stewart's writing must have been as clear and refreshing as spring rain.

The *Sketches* is in four parts, each with its particular value. Part 1 has been most heavily plundered by posterity. This is a study of the old Highland way of life, the clan system, and its destruction after the Rising of 1745. It is preceded by a map showing the territory held by the various clans. Delightful footnotes abound, going off on whatever tangent interested the author: Basques wearing the Highland bonnet, on the Gaelic of Connaught, the diplomatic skills of the chiefs, the gentleman highwayman of Badenoch, the lack of need for keys and locks. He examines the geography, the clan system, the arms, the garb, the music, the means of subsistence, and then the reasons for the Rising and its results.

Part 2 was the most controversial at the time. This is the *Present State and Changes of Character, Manners, and Personal Appearance*. Its theme is the alienation of the chiefs from their people. He discusses and illustrates this and writes of the decline in moral standards. Its cause? 'The system of modern Highland improvement marked by an aversion, inveterate as it seems unaccountable and causeless, to the ancient inhabitants, their customs, language, and garb. [It] will probably root out the language of the country, together with a great proportion of the people who speak it'.[144] And it 'can never be for the well-being of any state to deteriorate the character of, or to extirpate a brave, loyal, and moral people, its best supporters in war, and the most orderly, contented and economical in peace'.[145]

This is the section which singled out the Sutherland Clearances for condemnation but its sting must have been felt by large numbers of the land-owning classes in the Highlands. It could be different, he argues. Highlanders are adept at living on their unproductive land and, introduced slowly to improvements, their rents could be increased and there would be less risk to the proprietor than in leasing their land to the capital-rich sheep farmers who can easily go bankrupt.

He ends with a declaration of modesty, the only insincere passage in the book: 'I trust I shall not be thought presumptuous in making this feeble attempt, founded on a long intimacy with the people, both as inhabitants of their native glens, and as soldiers in barracks and in the field, and on some knowledge of the state of the country – to show what they were, what they now are, and what, under proper management, they may yet become'.[146]

Part 3 is the *Military Annals of the Highland Regiments*. He discusses each regiment and its wars from the embodiment of the Black Watch in 1740 through the fighting in Europe and the Americas. The anecdotage of the footnotes becomes even richer when he joins the campaigns in Flanders and, in the third edition, he ends the volume with an appendix.

Part 4, the second volume, deals with the Royal Highland Regiment, the Black Watch, through to Waterloo, and continues with the story of the other Highland regiments. It is enriched by a wealth of tiny detail intended to illustrate the excellence of his compatriots. He discusses punishment and drunkenness, privation, and adds pithy observations such as 'Few things increase a man's speed more effectually than the terror of a bayonet or a bullet in his rear'.[147]

He then has his section on the Fencibles and discusses the mutinies of the Highland regiments in the previous century (an appendix in the first edition) which are all put down to bad commanders. He finishes with lists of officers of the Highland regiments and details of their casualties. In the first edition this is where he places the main appendix. Parts 3 and 4 are virtually the only source for any study of these regiments before the wars against France and, even for those campaigns, it is often the best source.

The appendix consists of footnotes which were too long, even for the author, to remain footnotes. In the second and third editions, when it is placed at the end of the second volume, it contains 35 of these essays on subjects ranging through second sight, Highland weddings, a murder on Loch Tay, education and handwriting, Rob Roy, surnames, ghosts, and crimes and sentences in the northern counties. In one of them, BB, he illustrates his theme.

'To offer an agricultural comparison taken from a Highland glen, may occasion a smile; but I may be permitted to mention the relative state of two glens high up in the Highlands, both of nearly the same extent and quality of pasture and arable land, with no difference in climate. The one is full of people, all of whom are supported by the produce. The other glen was once as populous, but is now laid out in extensive grazings, and the arable land turned into pasture. The population of the latter, compared with the former, is as one to fifteen, and the difference in rent supposed to be about four per cent in favour of the stock farming glen. But in the populous district, the surface is cleared, the soil improved, and the produce increased, merely by the strength of many hands, without expense to the landlord either in building houses or otherwise. In the grazing glen the soil remains in a state of nature, and large sums have been expended in building houses for the men of capital. The income-tax being removed, few direct taxes reach them, horses or carts being scarcely at all employed; whereas, in the populous districts, taxes are paid for horses, hearths, dogs, and for the manufactures which the people consume. The stock-farmer ought to send more produce to market than can be spared, where there are so many people to support, but does this additional marketable produce go to the landlord?' Of course not.

The footnote is irresistible. 'It may not be irrelevant to state, that, notwithstanding the recent depopulation of the higher glens, their inhabitants have always been more athletic, better limbed, and more independent in their minds, than the inhabitants of the lower glens'. For David not only were Highlanders unquestionably superior to Lowlanders, but the higher the Highlander, the better.

He had intended to expand on the subject of discipline amongst troops 'but I gave up the idea, for the same reason that made me suppress many anecdotes and incidents which occurred in the course of my military duties, because I was myself often a party concerned, and unwilling to introduce my name, I found that, by stating the facts in the third person, much of the stamp of authenticity was lost'.[148]

He concludes his work with a modest disclaimer as to his abilities. 'I hope this attempt will at least show that the subject is worthy of some notice,' and, after giving a pretty acknowledgement to Walter Scott, he adds his qualifications for writing the book. He says he would not have considered disagreeing with 'men conspicuous for talents and acquirements, and to whose judgement I would readily yield, were I not sensible that I speak with more knowledge of facts illustrative of the subject, originating principally from the circumstances of my being a native of the country, and having from early infancy associated much with the people. Speaking their language, and keeping an attentive ear and observant eye to what was said and done in my presence, I have been enabled to acquire a considerable knowledge of their habits, dispositions, and traditional histories. Descended by both parents from families in which all I have said of patriarchal kindness and devoted attachment had for ages been exemplified with the happiest reciprocal results ... I should consider myself ungrateful and unworthy of that fidelity and friendship ... if I had not availed myself of those opportunities of calling the public attention to an interesting subject ... Having made use of these combined means of information when my profession offered no employment, I shall consider my spare time and humble talents as having been well occupied, if I have succeeded in affording some idea of the character, capability, and importance to the state, of an interesting part of the population'.[149]

The Highland Clearances are still raw in the Scottish psyche and the author of the *Sketches* presages the publishing industry – historical, poetical, popular, and dramatic – which is now devoted to them. 'We may look forward in that some person, capable of doing justice to so interesting a subject, will undertake it, and introduce many facts and much important information, which, in this first attempt to call the public attention to the state of the Highlands and the inhabitants, I have been induced, for various reasons, to suppress'.[150]

The first edition named the Marchioness of Stafford and discussed the trial on the charge of culpable homicide of her factor in Sutherland, Patrick Sellar. His 'acquittal did by no means diminish the general feeling of culpability; it only transferred the offence from the agent to a quarter too high and too distant to be directly affected by public indignation'. David also quoted the Sheriff-Substitute of Sutherland, Robert Mackid who described the Sutherland clearings as 'conduct which has seldom disgraced any country'.[151]

The author was ambivalent about this most controversial section of his work. 'I had some thoughts of omitting this part,' he had explained to Irvine, but said that he was 'under the control of my Commanding officers the Booksellers – whom I have consulted on this part, and they wont permit a line to be omitted'.[108] In the second edition this passage was slightly tweaked to make its impact even stronger, but then Sellar threatened legal action unless the section was changed.

This was no idle threat. Although the one-time factor had been abandoned by the Stafford family when he become an embarrassment, he had secured extensive leases in Sutherland and was now a rich grazier. He had already ruined Mackid, his principal accuser, who had faced a choice between bankruptcy or a letter of grovelling apology. Sellar was a cold, vindictive man and a dangerous opponent.

In the third edition Stewart removed the personal attacks but replaced them with a powerful condemnation, still clearly referring to the Sutherland clearers, of those who denigrated the character of the ancient inhabitants. This did not soften Sellar's opinion of the colonel whom he described as 'a selfish petty Highland laird who sees no further than the limits of the little sovereignty where Donald approaches him with fear and trembling – hunger in his face – a tattered philibeg of Stewart on his other end'.[152] A denunciation from such a quarter would have further boosted David's popularity amongst the mass of the Highlanders.

Even in 1822 Stewart was aware that the social revolution in the Highlands was not unique. Such upheavals have echoes many times in all societies. The agrarian improvements had already turned the peasants of England and southern Scotland into farm labourers for hire and then into workers in the new factories. The introduction of more efficient methods of production reduced the need for labour, then as now, and David's answer of splitting the land into countless small holdings to employ the population would receive as little favour today as it did from the Highland proprietors of the time.

And the Highlands were afflicted by too many catastrophes at one time for the social structure to survive. The clan system was already in decline before it was destroyed by the repression after the '45. Later in the eighteenth century and early in the next, great sums had been sunk into the region to create new industries and the infrastructure for them to thrive but the Industrial Revolution to the south undercut them as it also undercut the traditional rural craftsworkers.

In the south the dispossessed moved to nearby towns but there were no nearby towns in the Highlands. The people left the glens to earn their daily bread in the Glasgow manufactories. The Napoleonic War ended; young men could no longer join the army and perhaps send their wages home. The price of Highland produce fell back – first cattle, then sheep. The kelp industry, the one great hope for the future, was destroyed by the import of cheap foreign potash. Profits from its good years which could have been re-invested were dissipated by the landowners who were too often contemptuous of their people. And the country folk resented the changes and resisted co-operation with any of the lairds' improvements which might have given them a future.

The greatest catastrophe of all was the increase in population. In other times and other places people had to leave the land or face starvation but the potato – introduced by *Fear Ghart* to his estates in 1774 – allowed many more to pack the townships in abject poverty with no way to improve themselves. The logical outcome of Stewart's path would have been a revolution which wrested ownership of land from the lairds. Such an event would have resulted in the retention of a poverty-stricken peasantry in the Highlands and would have produced a very different society from today's.

The only other answer was emigration and the Highlander had been leaving his country in search of a better life for a century before Stewart's book and would continue to leave it for a century and a half to come. Sometimes the lairds tried to ban it; sometimes they encouraged it; sometimes they virtually took their redundant tenants by the scruff of the neck and hurled them into the holds of transatlantic ships. But hindsight can still offer no remedy to the Highland problem of the time and it still remains today.

Considering the furore raised by the Clearances and their outright condemnation by public opinion, it may seem surprising that the grossest injustices were not addressed until the Crofters Holdings (Scotland) Act of 1886. Even this was an unsatisfactory remedy. It broke what proprietors believed to be one of the foundations of the state by interposing a government mechanism between landlord and tenant which gave the remaining Highlanders security of tenure but it discouraged investment and froze the crofters on the marginal land to which they had been driven; the slow decline of the Highland economy would not be halted.

The *Sketches* came out in February 1822. Stewart wrote to Irvine on 11th April. 'Near 500 copies of my book were sold in London in the first six days, and a second edition is understandably called for, I must therefore go south as soon as possible and hurry the press, making only a few additions and corrections of style and arrangements, particularly as to the long and numerous notes – the question is whether to embody them in the text, or place them in the appendix – the necessity of keeping the book within a moderate size made me place so great a proportion in small types'.[153]

The reviews were highly favourable. 'This is really one of the most interesting books that has fallen under our notice for a long period,' said the *Edinburgh Evening Courant*, 'and embodies more authentic information regarding the former and present state of our northern countrymen than any work which has hitherto appeared ... it convincingly shows the fallacy of that system which, for a temporary increase to a rent roll, drives hosts of brave and attached dependents who can never be replaced to seek an asylum in distant lands ... The battle on the plains of Maida is delineated with equal effect: but the gallant author passes over with a modesty which we scarcely forgive him, the share he had in turning the tide of victory on that day.'

The *Sketches* is often described as a bestseller but this must be kept in context. Sir Walter Scott's *Fortunes of Nigel* was also published in 1822. Instead of 500 copies in a week, it sold 7,000 copies on its first day. Scott was writing himself out of debt, incurred by the collapse of the printer Ballantyne and Company which he had co-founded in 1809. He eventually paid the creditors at great cost to his health. At this stage Scott's debt amounted to £36,000. David Stewart's was £40,000. He was famous – always very important to him – but the financial future was little rosier.

CHAPTER SIXTEEN

The King's Jaunt

'One and twenty daft days'

IN AUGUST 1821 George IV visited Ireland. He had just been crowned after his long regency during his father's madness. The dissolute Prinny was now 59, a fat old man in poor health, addicted to cherry brandy and his mistress, the spectacularly endowed Marchioness of Conyngham. After Ireland he had also journeyed to the Continent at exorbitant cost to the Exchequer.

In 1822 he wished to visit Vienna to attend the Congress of Nations where he would meet the Tsar and the Emperor of Austria, but his ministers feared he would be vulnerable to the charms of the latter's chief minister, Metternich, whose diplomatic skills had shaped post-Napoleonic Europe. A less costly alternative, and one likely to be less disruptive to the country's foreign policy, would be a visit to Scotland which was already pencilled in his diary for 1823.

Rumours of this possible trip north had been circulating since the spring but the King preferred the idea of Vienna and a visit to Florence. The dangerous Radical tendency, with which the Duke of Atholl suspected David Stewart might be in sympathy, had recently led to strikes, riots, and executions in Scotland. The ruling classes in London had also been alarmed by the Cato Street Conspiracy which had planned the assassination of government ministers a few years earlier. These rumblings of discontent were used by the Foreign Secretary, Lord Londonderry, to persuade the King that the security of his realm demanded his presence in Scotland and thus make him the first monarch to visit the kingdom since Charles II.

In June, His Majesty was persuaded to drop his plan to attend the Congress but, although a notice of a likely visit was posted in the *Edinburgh Advertiser*, he was still reluctant to commit himself to a trip north. The confirmation came on 18th July in a letter to the Lord Provost of Edinburgh from the Lord Privy Seal for Scotland stating that the King would arrive in the city about 10th August.

'The announcement of this intelligence produced in Edinburgh an indescribable sensation, which was soon communicated to the remotest extremities of the kingdom,'[154] said a contemporary account, and, from all corners of the nation, people flocked to the capital.

In 1815, the Prince Regent had accepted the post of chieftain of the Highland Society of London and Walter Scott, created a baronet five years later, convinced His Highness that he was the true heir to Bonnie Prince Charlie and filled his head with the tartan flummery promoted by the Society. *Ossian, Waverley, The Lady of the Lake* occupied the King's vision of Scotland, not the growing urban slums, the Clearances, and the douce middle-class Lowlanders. So that he would not look out of place in his northern kingdom, His Majesty ordered a complete tartan outfit from George Hunter & Co of Princes Street which cost him £1,354 18s.

The Lord Provost turned to Sir Walter Scott for advice on how best to prepare for the forthcoming festivities and he set up a small committee to handle it. Two of its members, James Skene of Rubislaw and Alexander Keith of Ravelston, did not do a great deal but one did: David Stewart. And he was to do a lot of marching.

Along with his elder sister Clementina, still a spinster and still, in the words of her brother, 'of the tenderest and most humane disposition, with a heart that would not injure a fly,'[155] the colonel took a gig to the ferry at Logierait and caught the Caledonian Light Post Coach, southbound from Inverness, to Edinburgh. Another Drumcharry resident who made the trip was Duncan the Piper, 'Garth's Fool', one of the twins who had been raised in *Fear Ghart*'s kitchen. Duncan saw the king and pronounced him a *'duine reamhar tlachmhor'*, a fat handsome man.[156]

Two aspects in particular are remarkable about what Scott

called the 'King's Jaunt' – the astonishing frenzy of excitement into which it threw the citizens of Edinburgh and much of the rest of Scotland, and the pre-eminence in the festivities of the Highlander and the Highland Garb. David Stewart of Garth held a large share of responsibility for the latter.

The Highland Societies of Edinburgh and London were the oldest such institutions but organisations of similar intent had sprung up in places like Inverness, Dunkeld – and Madras. Ostensibly they were there to promote the culture of the Gael but, in an age when gentlemen – and those who aspired to this station – socialised by coming together in dining clubs, these societies gave an opportunity for members to dress up in tartan, sing sentimental songs, and drink very large amounts of claret and whisky.

The Celtic Society was one such. Based in Edinburgh it had been founded in January 1820 by David Stewart and William Mackenzie of Gruinard with Sir Walter Scott as its president. Its membership included many who were Highland aristocrats but its bulk was made up of the professional men of the city. In 1822 it was described as 'A body of about 80 or a hundred Highlanders and amateurs, associated for encouraging and reviving the national costume of the mountains, and numbering many men of rank and consequence'.

Sir Walter and his deputy decided to give the Society a leading role in the King's visit. David's history of the Highland Regiments, out for some six months, had given him unique prestige in the eyes of those thousands of his fellow countrymen who had fought in the war. The other parts of the *Sketches* had established him as the authority on the history and the customs of the Highlands. He was the arbiter on the correct form of Highland dress to be worn during the royal visit and was given the task of drilling and disciplining the Celts and the other Highland contingents who were due in town so that they would provide worthy escorts for the monarch.

The egregious Macdonell of Glengarry, surely jealous that David, the *Sketches* a success, was threatening his own position as the most Highland of Highlanders, and the Duke of Atholl pointed out that most members of the Celtic Society were 'amateurs', not proper Highlanders at all. Glengarry may even have noticed a thinly veiled attack upon his own behaviour in the *Sketches*. 'Gentlemen would be more honourably employed in individually removing the cause of the distress of the people – which they themselves have the power to do – than in calling public meetings in Edinburgh and other towns, to proclaim to the world the destitute and deplorable state of their dependents and tenants'.[157]

The capital took on a carnival air. People erected flags and banners and tradesmen vied with each other to create 'remarkable devices' tacked on to the frontage of their premises – tableaux which would be brilliantly illuminated with newfangled gas when the King arrived.

Summoned by Scott, more Highlanders poured into the city. Stewart's correspondent, Sir John Macgregor-Murray, had just died and the MacGregors were under their new chief. A party of Breadalbane's tenants arrived, many of whom were to turn out again some 20 years later to welcome Queen Victoria and her new husband to Taymouth and inspire them to buy Balmoral. The Drummonds came, led by Lord Gwydir, the Deputy Great Chamberlain of England. He was there in his capacity as husband of their chief for Lady Gwydir was the daughter of the late Earl of Perth and chatelaine of Drummond Castle. Under Stewart of Ardvorlich members of the Strathfillan Society appeared, as did Glengarry with two dozen of his Society of True Highlanders, and 50 rather scruffy tenants of Lady Stafford from Sutherland.

The first spectacle for the entertainment of the people took place on the lawns between Queen Street and Heriot Row. The sound of pipes drifting across the New Town each morning was the signal that Colonel Stewart was exercising the Celtic Society and the other Highlanders. Although no man was said to be able to embody a Corps like David he must have had his work cut out.

On Saturday 10th August, 'in the presence of many delighted

spectators', General William Stirling made a speech saying that a lady of distinguished rank could not be found in time to perform the task of presenting the two standards to the Celts, but Sir Walter Scott and Colonel Stewart of Garth, who 'give weight and honour to every thing they might undertake', were to do it. Scott made a pretty speech before presenting his standard; David held his tongue.

The breathless reporter described the Society members. 'In general, they are fully and even superbly dressed and arrayed in the belted plaid, each in his own clan tartan, which distinction gives a rich and half barbaric effect to their appearance. Their grenadiers carry partizans and targets, and are headed by Captain Mackenzie of Gruinard, whose stately, and at the same time handsome and active figure, realizes the *idea* of a complete Highland soldier. Here and there a white knee betrays a Southron or Lowlander – in most the limb is as dark as that of Glune-dhu (Black Knee) himself'.

But the King was yet to arrive. 'As day after day elapsed, hope, fear, and anxiety began to distract the public mind'. This was partially assuaged on the following Monday – the 12th – when the crown and the rest of the Scottish regalia which had been unearthed in a trunk inside the castle by Sir Walter in 1815 were marched down the High Street to the palace of Holyroodhouse, so that they could be marched back up the hill in the presence of the King.

First the Highlanders paraded on Heriot Row where they swore the oath of allegiance. Then they marched up to the top of the Mound and joined others of the escort before moving onto the esplanade in front of the Castle. When the regalia emerged they were borne through cheering throngs down to Holyroodhouse. David and the Celts followed the trumpeter and an advance guard of Yeomanry. Alone in a coach, Scott came next. Then came another four dignitary-stuffed carriages, the crown and its accessories, the MacGregors and, finally, more mounted yeomanry. David had trod the cobbled High Street in such a parade seven years earlier with the Black Watch. He would not have acknowledged the cheers, concentrating, 'in his usual earnest way',[158] on the drill of his men and the seriousness of the occasion.

Nothing happened on the Tuesday. Once again the only action took place at Queen Street where David drilled the Highlanders. But on Wednesday morning the *Royal George* was sighted in the Firth of Forth. Cannon on Calton Hill boomed the signal and the city was suddenly filled with archers, heralds, Highlanders, soldiers, and magistrates all holding onto their hats and hurrying to their appointed positions for the march down to Leith to welcome their monarch. With an estimated one seventh of the population of Scotland lining the shore and cheering, the King sailed into the port and cast anchor in time for his luncheon. The Royal Salute was fired and the Edinburgh crowds rushed to their vantage points along the route.

The weather being damp and inclement, His Majesty decided to shelter on board for the rest of the day but he came up to the deck to view the boats filled with people who sailed out to look at him. He lowered a bottle of claret to a steamboat and its passengers drank his health. He invited Sir Walter to dinner.

On Thursday the rain ceased and the King decided to land at midday. The Celtic Society mustered in Queen Street at nine o'clock and fitted themselves into the long cavalcade of spectacularly dressed luminaries. Near the back, sandwiched between the Knight Marischal and his attendants – 'mounted on beautiful horses, caparisoned with white and gold lace' – and a division of Scots Greys, marched David in command of the second company of Celts. They were all down at Leith docks by 11 am, trying to sort themselves into order for the return trip with the King. Glengarry who had found himself a horse jostled for position with the Celts by the royal coach.

The King landed and was greeted by the VIPs. Cannon roared the salute, thousands cheered, Glengarry made a nuisance of himself and everyone returned up Leith Walk. David now had most of the Celtic Society under his command and he was near the head of the column with two pipers, hard on the hooves of the Scots Greys, and being cheered by 'incalculable multitudes'.

Halfway up Leith Walk, they passed the toll house upon which were the words 'Descendant of the immortal Bruce, thrice welcome!' His Majesty, whose behaviour could not be faulted throughout the visit, perused it with 'marked emotion'.

Everyone stopped while the Lord Provost waved the city keys on a velvet cushion beneath the royal nose. Then they continued through St Andrew's Square to Princes Street where the view inspired the King with 'sensations of delight and astonishment' and he said "How superb!"' On seeing the crowd lining the hill beneath the Old Town, 'His Majesty recoiled, if we may use the term, with wonder at the sight, but instantly looked up again, and betrayed in his countenance the deepest emotion'. They marched on to Holyroodhouse where the King disembarked. Cannon bellowed out from the Castle and from a battery on Salisbury Crags when His Majesty crossed the threshold of the palace.

Amongst the hundreds of thousands of Scots who watched the procession, not one was seen to be drunk, not one committed a crime, and there was not one 'whose behaviour would have been offensive in a private drawing-room'. This celebration of national identity and the Act of Union had the support of everyone although a few cavilled sourly at the omnipresence of the Highlanders who, after all, represented only a small, semi-barbaric segment of the population. The King sat on his throne and received addresses until half-past three when he boarded a closed coach and thundered off with an escort of Greys to Dalkeith House. Lord Montague on behalf of his nephew and ward, the young Duke of Buccleuch, lent the mansion to the King and his attendants for the duration of the visit. That evening David Stewart dined with Sir Walter Scott in Castle Street.

CHAPTER SEVENTEEN

God bless the Land of Cakes!

'A vera pretty man'

NOTHING MUCH HAPPENED on Friday. The King remained at Dalkeith and the crowds on the streets of Edinburgh enjoyed decorous celebrations and did the rounds of the illuminations after dark. At 10 pm the guns all went off – from the Castle, Calton Hill, Salisbury Crags, at Leith, and from the ships anchored offshore. The 13th and the 66th Regiment fired their muskets in the gaps between the louder bangs.

On Saturday afternoon the King held a levee at the Palace where the ruling class of the nation queued up to be presented. David was in the anteroom beforehand, adjusting his monarch's spanking new tartans, weaponry, Highland jewels, and ensuring the straightness of the seams on the flesh-coloured silk tights that encased the royal legs. He finally was satisfied, declaring the King 'a vera pretty man'.[159] The kit boggled the minds of His Majesty's Scots subjects but they had little time to register it as they passed in front of him at a rate of fifteen per minute. Colonel Stewart joined in this parade, and himself presented a Lieutenant McNivin, once in the 42nd but now of the 26th regiment.

By half-past four the King was rumbling back to Dalkeith and he stayed there throughout Sunday. He tore himself away for a couple of hours at Holyrood on Monday afternoon to receive loyal addresses and was back there the following day in the palace drawing room to meet 'five hundred ladies of the most distinguished rank, fashion, and beauty in Scotland'.

Clementina was amongst them. This is the sole reference to her during the fortnight. It is likely she was in charge of her brother's Highland garb, ensuring his brogues and his shirt were always clean, his silver sword well polished, and that his plaid was dried out after the frequent soakings it received when its owner was marching round the city or waiting on the King.

David must have pulled strings to have her presented by the Duchess of Atholl. Clemmie was not a lady of the most distnguished rank. She was the 52-year-old spinster daughter of a debt-ridden Highland laird. Fashionable she cannot have been and, if beautiful, she was unique in a family whose portraits show many sterling qualities but little comeliness. The diarist James Robertson described Jessie's granddaughter, Sophie, as 'a very plain child and like the Garths'. Clementina was one of a batch of 51 ladies run past His Majesty by the Duchess. All wore their ostrich plumes, best dresses and jewels, but Clemmie's frock was not one that the reporters singled out for mention.

The King took Wednesday off and arrived at Holyrood on Thursday afternoon for another of Sir Walter's bits of pageantry. This time His Majesty was joined by the regalia for a trip up the High Street to the Castle and back again. There were some 35 elements to the procession which was 'splendid without being gaudy'. David was near the front commanding the Celtic Society, the first of the Highlanders.

The crowd was as rapturously ecstatic as it always was and the ladies lining the route 'were most condescendingly acknowledged by His Majesty'. The King clambered up to the castle's Half Moon Battery and, a tiny, plump figure scarcely visible in the mist and rain, took off his field-marshal's cocked hat and waved it to the crowds far below. He then took a glass of wine before the glittering assembly wound its way back to the Palace via a detour down the Mound into Princes Street. Our reporter records that 'His Majesty had actually got wet' although his closed carriage would have left him not half so wet as everyone else. He was then whisked back to Dalkeith for a stiff drink before dinner with his cronies.

Friday the 23rd turned out a nice day for the grand cavalry review which was to take place on Portobello Sands. Commanded by the King to turn out with the Celtic Society and the other Highlanders, David paraded them as usual in Queen Street before handing over to the Duke of Argyll who led the whole Highland contingent on the long march to Portobello.

They lined up on the sands waiting patiently while the cavalry performed their evolutions before the monarch who raised his hat and bowed to each officer. Then the crowd, 50,000 on this occasion, broke through the cordon of horsemen and isolated the Highlanders from His Majesty who forgot about them. A message was passed through to him and he graciously waited in his carriage while the Celts, many of them city folk past the flush of youth, trudged past through sand pitted with hoofprints. The sovereign then rumbled his way back to Dalkeith and the Highlanders followed the Duke of Argyll to his house in George Street where they were dismissed.

There was a ball in the Assembly Rooms that evening, a Highland ball because that is what people knew the King enjoyed. And he did. Rather than take the throne prepared for him, he took a position in the middle of the room and 'frequently looked up to the band with a smile of satisfaction and snapped his fingers'.

The monarch had a powerful effect on his musicians. Nathaniel Gow, son of Niel and a great virtuoso himself, had played after dinner in Dalkeith House two days before. The King proposed a banally flattering toast which quite overcame the player. He was heard to utter the words 'I'm perfectly content to die now!' His Britannic Majesty watched the reels for half an hour, and was observed to 'seize hold of the Duke of Atholl and Lord Melville, and draw them away to a considerable distance' before leaving for Dalkeith at 11.15. The Ball went on until 7 am.

The following morning, once more in close proximity to the backsides of the horses of the Scots Greys, David was marching again. Still the cheering crowds lined the streets. This time he was plodding up the slippery cobbles of the High Street from Holyrood, acting as escort to the crown and its accoutrements – the Honours of Scotland – for their return to the castle. His second engagement of the day – and the King's first – was a banquet in the Great Hall of Parliament House given by the Lord Provost and the Town Council of Edinburgh, at which 303 men, noble and gentle, were guests. Chiefs wore their tartan. His Majesty arrived at quarter past six and was in 'excellent spirits'.

Our reporter lists the menu. On the King's right was Lord Errol and *Escalopes de Poulets a l'Essence*. On his left was the Lord Provost and *Sauté de Grouse aux Truffes*. The handiest puddings for His Majesty were *Gelée de Vin* and *Chartreuse d'Abricot*. He partook of some turtle and grouse soups for his starter, then stewed carp, venison, and a little grouse, and finished with apricot tart. He drank moselle, a little champagne and then settled in to the claret.

The band played Scottish airs, and although it was 'impossible by words to convey an adequate idea of the grace and dignity of His Majesty's manner on the occasion of the banquet', he was clearly delighted with 'The Cameronian's Rant', for 'besides beating time to it with his hands, he accompanied the air with the most rapid inclinations of his person'. He even condescended to join in the singing of *Non nobis Domine* after dinner and 'his voice, which is a very fine bass, was distinctly heard'.

After the food the loyal toast was drunk, which was the signal for two rockets to soar skyward, themselves triggering salutes from the Castle, Calton Hill, Salisbury Crags, and the warships anchored off Leith. His Majesty dubbed the Lord Provost a baronet and the newly created Sir William Arbuthnott fell to his knees to kiss the majestic hand. The King's toast was not to the nation but to 'all chieftains and all the clans of Scotland, and may God bless the Land of Cakes!' At 9 pm, after another five toasts, his own drunk with 'three times three, which were timed by His Majesty himself, and followed up by the most enthusiastic plaudits', he left for Dalkeith.

The company remained to drink further toasts – Sir Walter's 'Both sides of St George's Channel', the Duke of Atholl's 'May the radiant *Sun* of Royalty see what the *Sons* of Scotland are made of (*Loud applause*)', Lord Ashburton's 'The author of Waverley, whoever he may be, and his works' – Glengarry made a fiery speech, the Duke of Hamilton made a bad one. The Hon. Capt. Napier, R.N. ticked off the Duke of Atholl for depressing the

God bless the Land of Cakes! 145

company with a toast to the late Mr Pitt, and himself proposed 'The Baronet of Renfrew, and the Yeomanry of Scotland, with such men old mother Caledonia would live for ever'. All in all 43 toasts were drunk, each of which demanding that glasses were drained. The party broke up six and a half hours after it first sat down.

On Sunday the King — and David Stewart — attended divine service in the High Church of St Giles. As far as the crowds were concerned, 'Great as their exultation must have been to behold their sovereign in the midst of them, the sentiment of piety alone predominated ... When the royal carriage was near the Cross, a few boys took off their hats, as if about to cheer His Majesty; but some old men dissuasively held up their hands, and the most prompt obedience was yielded to their signal. This circumstance was much noticed by the King'.

His Majesty, more used to the practices of the Church of England, was enthroned before the pulpit and in no position to judge correct form by following the actions of the other worshippers. 'The officiating minister on this occasion was Dr Lamont, the moderator of the General Assembly, who commenced the service by giving out the first version of the 100th psalm. His Majesty lifted a psalm book, and stood during the reading; and his example was followed by the rest of the congregation'. He retired to Dalkeith for lunch.

On Monday the monarch made a private tour of Holyroodhouse. In the evening was another ball, the Caledonian Hunt Ball, in the Assembly Rooms. His Majesty in his uniform of Colonel of the Guards arrived fifteen minutes earlier than he had at the Peers Ball, but maintained impartiality by also leaving fifteen minutes earlier. David Stewart was there. The King had asked for 'an abundance of Scots reels and strathspeys. "I dislike," said His Majesty, "seeing any thing in Scotland that is not purely national and characteristic."' Quadrilles were restricted to the second ballroom.

On Tuesday morning the sovereign had been expected to attend the laying of the foundation stone for the National Monument but he stayed indoors. The ceremony was carried out by the Freemasons whose ranks contained the most powerful men in Scotland. Colonel Stewart was there. In September 1821 he is 'recorded in the register of the Supreme Grand Royal Arch Chapter of Scotland, as having been regularly Exalted to the Royal Arch Degree'. He owned a very natty silk apron painted with roses, cherubs, and kilted pipers. The Masons were joined in Parliament Square by dragoons and the Greys and, each lodge carrying its banner, they marched from Parliament Square to Calton Hill, 'where the multitude assembled was prodigious'. The great men made speeches – long speeches – and the foundation stone was laid above a time capsule. Then they marched back to Freemasons Hall and dispersed. Sadly, funds ran out and the monument is still to be completed. It has been dubbed 'Scotland's Disgrace'.

Sir Walter was not present at this occasion. He had gone for tea with the King at Melville Castle. His Majesty viewed the Mid-Lothian cavalry, and the most 'elegant refection was prepared, consisting of pastry, ices, fruits &c, and a great variety of the choicest wines. The King expressed himself highly gratified with the splendour of the preparations, but declined partaking'. He left for home at half-past four whereupon the rest of the company sat down and partook.

After dinner His Majesty went to the Theatre Royal at the top of Leith Walk for a performance of *Rob Roy*. 'It would be impossible to calculate the crowds which thronged and choked up every approach to the theatre ... Several gentlemen fainted ... In the pit and galleries the audience were so closely wedged together that it would have been found difficult to introduce between any two even the point of a sabre ... The boxes were filled with the rank, wealth, and beauty of Scotland. In this dazzling galaxy we observed the gallant Sir David Baird, Colonel Stewart of Garth, Glengarry, the Lord Provost, and Sir Walter Scott; each of whom, as he entered, was greeted with loud acclamation'. It is recorded that none were cheered louder than Colonel Stewart.[160] One hopes he took along Clemmie.

The audience waited for two hours in a high good humour, singing comic Scottish songs and an 'Auld lang syne'. The King's carriage thundered up to the portico at ten past eight and the audience greeted him with a 'prolonged and heartfelt shout which for more than a minute rent the house ... His Majesty, with his wonted affability, repeatedly bowed to the audience, while the kindly smile which beamed from his manly countenance expressed to this favoured portion of his loving subjects the regard with which he viewed them'. During the performance the sovereign's appreciation 'was by no means a "stage-box simper," but a hearty sonorous laugh, such as belongs only to a frank and generous nature'.

Our reporter neglects to advise us of the time of His Majesty's departure, perhaps because he was occupied strapping himself to the royal coach since he is able to tell us that the monarch, on the way back to Dalkeith, 'laughed very much in his carriage at the wit of the Bailie, and observed that the play was neither too long nor too short, and that he was quite delighted with it'.

David Stewart, and perhaps Clemmie, went on to another ball in the Assembly Rooms, this time under the patronage of several ladies of the most exalted rank. The King hosted a Highland dinner party, drinking 'Atholl brose, which had become His Majesty's most common beverage at table, and to which he declared himself partial'.

On the last day of the Jaunt the King journeyed to Hopetoun House for luncheon with the Earl and his Countess. The indigenous inhabitants of the district turned out by the thousand to view him, and, entertained by the Royal Company of Archers, enjoyed a *fête champêtre* in the rain. Inside 'His Majesty ate sparingly of turtle soup, and drank three glasses of wine during his repast'. He then knighted Henry Raeburn and Captain Adam Ferguson, Keeper of the Regalia.

His Majesty left Hopetoun at quarter-past three to join the royal yacht which was waiting at Queensferry. 'An immense assemblage' was there to cheer. The majestic countenance was observed to wear an air of melancholy and 'he never once smiled from the time of leaving his carriage'. His final act of affability was in being 'particularly pleased by the appearance of Captain Munro Ross and several of his friends, completely and elegantly equipped in their native tartan' who sailed round the *Royal George* with a piper who had difficulty maintaining his footing in the swell. His Majesty half suspected that he 'had been making too free with the Glenlivet'. He almost certainly had.

George IV was self-indulgent, frivolous, and dissipated, which affected not one whit the deference shown to him by his Scots subjects. In preparing for an event such as the 1822 visit today, the wishes of a constitutional monarch would not be paramount but Scott designed the Jaunt to meet the King's expectation of Scotland and he believed it to be a country of tartan-clad Highlanders. His Majesty and the overwhelming mass of the Scottish nation loved it. Our reporter considered one of the greatest benefits of the Jaunt to be the love rekindled in the bosoms of the people for their aristocracy, previously considered remote and anglicised, but now seen as upholders of the native traditions and ceremonies. It was more.

The Jaunt was a highly successful celebration of the Treaty of Union. Beyond that the pageantry mounted by Sir Walter took the fancy of his countrymen. Their imaginations were stimulated by the Highlanders who had been welded into an impressive and disciplined body under David's direction. The Lowland spectators decided to claim this romantic version of Gaeldom as their own heritage, an appropriation further cultivated by the Victorians. It had little to do with reality but served as a powerful focus for national pride which assisted the Scottish identity to survive the overwhelming proximity of its larger neighbour.

Stewart was second only to Scott in creating this Highland self-image for their countrymen. In John Prebble's opinion, 'More than any other man, even Scott, he [Stewart] was responsible for the conventional and enduring picture of the Highland clansman and soldier'. David collected the first tartans. He was the first to describe Highland society. He turned the myths of Ossian and Scott into reality — his own highly partial, romantic reality — and sold it to the nation. Perhaps it was largely bogus but this permits it to change and evolve, adopting fresh tartans and fresh adherents worldwide. The Duke of Atholl, so often a discordant note in the background of David Stewart's life, may have described the Jaunt as 'one and twenty daft days' but, for good or ill – mostly good – the image which David played so large a part in creating still largely identifies his nation to itself as well as to the world.

CHAPTER EIGHTEEN

Fame but no Fortune

*'At one Publick dinner I sat only four from the
Duke of Sussex'*

THE STEWARTS did not stay long in Edinburgh after the King had departed. David was now laird but it changed little. He had been running the estates for more than a year and the crushing load of debt had not eased. He took no part in the public backbiting after the King's visit. Glengarry rushed to the correspondence columns of Blackwood's Magazine, spluttering his doubts about the authenticity of the Celtic Society with his usual mixture of arrogance and bile.

In a letter asking for Scott's approval for a petition seeking the King's patronage of the Celtic Society, the colonel poured out his dislike of the man. 'He does infinite injury to his poor countrymen in the false and erroneous views he offers to the public of what he is pleased to call a True Highlander ... Had it not been for Glengarry the King's visit would have passed without an angry word or unpleasant feeling ... I see Glengarry continues his attempt to bring odium on the Highland character by instituting premiums for such brutal feats as that of twisting off the leg of a cow. With tolerable knowledge of Highland customs I declare I never heard even a hint of such a savage and useless exhibition of strength'.[161]

David was also seeking expert advice. Whilst in Edinburgh, he had done the rounds of the booksellers trying to collect money from his sales. 'I came back without the receipt of a shilling altho they have sold 1800 copies of my book. I know not what kind principles regulate the conduct of booksellers in general, but those I have to deal with seem to entertain very different views of fair dealing from what I have been accustomed to practice as a soldier'.

As always, people expected a published work to produce a cascade of wealth for its author. 'Little did your ancestors dream that the land they had acquired with their swords should by one of their descendants be rescued with the pen,'[162] wrote a widow from Elgin. In fact Stewart received £159 2s 10d as his share of the profits of the first edition, and an advance of £300 for the 1200 copies of the 2nd. The third – 750 copies – was printed in 1824. These sums made little impression on the £40,000 debt. The widow, Mrs Gordon, also pointed out that the King's visit had made him 'altogether a public character ... That would have been the time to have asked for an appointment with the India Government or anything you wished for'.

He must have thought of that but he was being pressed in other directions. He had scattered complimentary copies of his book parsimoniously – to the Highland Society of London, Lord Chandos, Lord Dalhousie and a couple of advocate friends. One went to the Duke of Clarence, who would succeed his brother to the throne as William IV and he sent back 'five pages close written in his own hand ... expressing the most unqualified approbation of my book'.[161] His Royal Highness wrote that he had 'read the book with great pleasure' and suggested the 'British Army must be upheld and the mind of the country turned to Military pursuits for which purpose I most strongly recommend your undertaking this work of elucidating the history of the British Army'.[163]

David felt such a task 'would be too great an undertaking for me'. He did dabble with a history of the Stewart family and he started collecting material for a definitive work about the Rising of 1745 which Constable hoped to publish. Home's *History of the Rebellion* was the standard work and its creator spent many summers in the Highlands collecting material from Jacobite families and survivors of the Rising. Much disappointment was expressed at the book when it was published. David put down the cause to an accident which befell the author. 'In travelling through Ross-shire, his carriage was overturned and he received a severe contusion on the head, which had such an effect on his nerves, that both his memory and judgement were very considerably affected ever after'.[164] After some research the colonel came to the conclusion that the Rising was still too painful a subject to be discussed as he wished and he dropped the idea. But he was promoting the Sketches as hard as he could. Its royalties might not clear his debts but it brought his name before persons of influence, which was critical if he was to resume the career for which he hankered.

During the royal visit he had endeared himself to Lady Gwydir, chief of the Drummonds, and afterwards corresponded with her in Brighton where her husband was one of the King's inner circle. David asked for her opinion of his book. In replying she passed on smatterings of court gossip. Although useful round the dinner tables of Highland Perthshire this was not quite what he wanted. He must have given a broader hint in his next letter, for Lady Gwydir responds with better detail: 'I had the honour of being three times with His Majesty last week, & I assure you he is quite enthusiastic in his admiration of the Highlanders, he seldom conversed on any other subject more than five minutes always revisiting his favourite theme, from after dinner to half past eleven the hour for withdrawing'.[165]

That was better, but still not quite enough. By her third letter, Lady Gwydir quite understood what was required of her. 'From the King's conversation I never entertained a doubt that all his minute & extraordinary information was derived from your work, but as His Majesty said we are to go to the Pavilion soon. I will take an opportunity of asking him, & I will not fail to inform you, tho I was so persuaded of it that I did not ask him'.

In the spring of 1823, just after impregnating 27-year-old Christian McLean, David left Drumcharry for London. He was looking for a rich wife and jobhunting both for himself and for Sandy Irvine, the minister's eldest son, who was now 17. He spent a day or two in Edinburgh before catching a ship to the Thames and had time to canvass the offer of a legal apprenticeship for his nephew but its cost proved prohibitive.

He took rooms in Mount Street but matters did not go well. 'The most important business I have on hand in my negotiations with Miss B which I much fear will end in nothing'.[166] Miss B is later named by Mrs Robertson of Kindrochet as 'Miss Bruce'. The only apparent candidate was Mary Agnew Bruce, daughter of Sir William Bruce bt. She married in 1828 when she was 30 and could have been sufficiently shelf-bound three years earlier to consider a much respected colonel – even if he was 50, debt-ridden, and battle-scarred.

David's search for an appointment went no better. 'I am very busy here, doing nothing that is, nothing in so far as what goes to procure money or an increase of fortune but as to attention, personal respect, and esteem to my name and character I meet with what is to me quite surprising, and being unlooked for and unexpected it is the more pleasing. From the Royal Family downwards I find the same and I could fill sheets to tell you all – but then to think that all the estates must be sold, and the family and name extinct, is a sad damper – but this I must endeavour to prevent'.

He could not resist exulting in his social success. The letter is to his brother-in-law, son of a tenant, who was to pass his entire adult life as a minister in the Highlands. If he did not drop the names about Dunkeld and Birnam his wife must have done.

'I met Lady Stafford at a Gala lately,' wrote David. 'She made up to me without any introduction, and was most gracious – so much so, that all those who knew us both and had read my book were surprised – as I was – the book has occasioned a strong sensation and impression most favourable to Scotland in this town – I was at a Scotch ball on Monday. The Duke and Duchess of Clarence, the Duchess of Kent, the Duke and Duchess of Gloucester, Prince Leopold – a long list of nobility, with 950 ladies and gentlemen were present – I was asked to begin the Ball which I did with the D of Montrose's daughter. At one Publick dinner I sat only four from the Duke of Sussex in the Chair and at another I was placed the fifth from the Duke of Clarence (on these occasions the principal people present are arranged in their places by the Stewards) and had particular attention paid me – all this is very gratifying, and I only want money to enable me to hold my station in such society'.

Irvine had told him of further clearances by the Duke of Atholl and David did not mince his words. He did not have to since this was part of the letter that the minister would never have dared to pass on.

'The account you give of the D of Athole's doings is quite deplorable – If all landlords were equally grinding and cruel oppressors as the Duke you would in a few years have your parishioners Irishmen – burning houses, murdering, and giving public orders to pay neither rents nor ministers stipends and denouncing all who offered to pay – Such is the state of the district where Colonel Dick of the 42nd is now, and such will be the state of all Athole if all landlords act like the Duke of that once respectable district, peopled by a brave, moral and independent race of men – Oppression has been the cause of the Irish disorders and as surely will the same effect be brought about by the same cause in the highlands ... If you will write a few facts of what is passing in Athole with a few observations – short but pithy and to the point, I will get them inserted in the newspapers here – the Duke is considered a great Patriot and most indulgent landlord in this town'.

Stewart intended to return north by August, but 'the truth is I am not anxious to be at Drumcharry that month as people would be coming then, and I am neither in spirits or in a proper state to entertain visitors – Had I sufficient address to get a wife, and interest to get a lucrative situation I might then be in a condition to receive visitors – With the prospect of seeing all the estate in the market before eight months It would be absurd to attempt to keep a house'. The minister's wife, Jessie, was unwell and her brother recommended she convalesce at Fortingall. 'She must go to Drumcharry and remain there till I go home. I need not call it home – It will soon be home to some other more fortunate and richer person'.

Captain Duncan Robertson of Kindrochet was with his regiment in Ireland which meant that his wife was passing local news on to him. 'Col David was expected in Edinburgh this week, but I have not been able to learn whether he came or not, his acquaintances say he has been unsuccessful in his suit with Miss Bruce, and also in his application for the Governorship of some of the West India Islands which he was making all the interest he could find and which at his time of life I really wonder he would take altho it was offered to him'.[167]

Written by a clerk – with corrections in David's hand – a record survives of one of the visitors to his rooms off Grosvenor Square. 'GRATITUDE AND DISINTERESTED ATTACHMENT' is its headline, with suitable curlicues to the script. 'Charles Stewart, born on the estate of Garth in the Highlands of Perthshire, has resided near forty years in London; but though so long absent from his native glens, he appears to have preserved one characteristic trait for which the inhabitants have long been distinguished. He called upon me some weeks ago, and sat for a considerable time anxiously inquiring for his old acquaintance and recalling to his recollection many circumstances of his earlier years. When he rose up to take his leave I said I was certain he would grieve to learn that my father and brother had left their affairs in such a situation that a great portion of the estate must be sold. He was standing close to the door, which he had opened to walk out, but when he heard me he shut it hastily and in an agitated tone exclaimed "What did you say Sir, do I understand you properly, must the land of your forefathers go from you?" I answered that I was afraid it must be so."Sir, Sir," said he, "it cannot be, it must not be so. You must not part with those lands on which your ancestors were for so many ages, the kind landlords, the protectors of my forefathers. I have three hundred pounds at command for which I will run home instantly. I have near four thousand pounds in the three percents, which I will draw at settling day. The whole is yours – pay me when you please. It is enough for me that I am able to assist the descendant of the honoured protectors of my relations and family."'[168]

CHAPTER NINETEEN

A Country Gentleman

'I am not in the habit of either forming or joining in conspiracies'

FOR THE NEXT few years the colonel remained at Drumcharry under the shadow of his debts living the life of a country gentleman. His aim was still to salvage his father's reputation by paying off all the liabilities and the estates were exposed to the market but with the downturn in agriculture they did not attract an adequate bid. His creditors understandably believed that they had a better chance of being paid if they kept him on the lands for, as long as he should live, his sense of honour would ensure that their interests and interest were paramount.

Of course he became busy, taking on the directorship of the County and City of Perth Fire Insurance Company, becoming a Deputy Lieutenant for Weem, a Commissioner of Supply, Justice of the Peace, a member of the Perthshire Hunt. He was appointed Substitute Grand Principal of the Grand Chapter of Royal Arch Free Masons of Scotland, a director of the Scottish Military and Naval Academy and, having judged the piping competition in 1825, he became chieftain of the St Fillan's Highland Society two years later.

When the Excise Act of 1823 was passed, making the landlord responsible for illegal stills found on his property, Stewart began a legal distillery at Tynadalloch, adjacent to the busy mill and smithy at Keltneyburn. His two main local interests seem to have been the improvement of local roads and the establishment of *quoad sacra* parishes. He was primarily responsible for the creation of the churches at Foss and Innerwick in Glen Lyon which were both carved out of the vastness of the parish of Fortingall.

Heritors, the proprietors of heritable land, were responsible for upkeep of the roads and also for installing ministers and ensuring the parish church was kept in order. Unlike many of his fellow lairds, David took a keen interest in both duties.

In 1814, the government ceased to maintain the military roads in the Highlands and devolved the cost of upkeep to the Highland counties. Perthshire refused to incur the expense and, for ten years, Wade's roads were left to decay. By 1824 the route from Crieff to Dalnacardoch crossing Tay and Tummel Bridges was virtually impassable to wheeled traffic, so the colonel took it upon himself to organise meetings with the other proprietors to repair it. They had it surveyed by Telford and by Joseph Mitchell, superintendent of the parliamentary roads.[169]

In his old age Mitchell wrote about his days in the Highlands and produces a vignette of David Stewart with whom he stayed at Drumcharry. He describes 'The dear old Colonel ... a bluff soldier ... an authority in the literary world on account of his book ... universally beloved, particularly by the common people ... no man knew them better or had greater influence with them'. He was 'a rambling speaker, and it is said that at the feast after his father's funeral, when the memory of the deceased was drunk, the Colonel got up to return thanks, and assured the numerous assemblage that "if the old gentleman, the deceased, was then present he was sure he would make them all very welcome."' [170]

Mitchell also mentions Clementina. 'Colonel Stewart had a maiden sister who lived with him, and who possessed all the generous and unselfish aspirations peculiar to the best of her sex ... In the evenings, he would send for three or four young lads, tenants' sons who were expert fiddlers, and thus he would have two or three hours of most excellent Scotch airs, reels, and strathspeys'.

The colossus of fiddle music was Niel Gow from Inver by Dunkeld. Initially patronised by the Duke of Atholl, by his death in 1807 he had become famous throughout Britain and his tradition was continued by his sons and other musicians, many from Highland Perthshire. These men were prolific composers and often named their airs after celebrated Scots or their patrons – the lairds and their womenfolk.

One would expect to see tunes named after David Stewart, especially after the publication of the *Sketches*, but the run of compositions in his honour is particularly satisfying. 'Capt David Stewart 42nd Royal Highlander's Reel' was composed by Malcolm McDonald of Dunkeld, cellist to Niel Gow. 'Major David Stewart's Strathspey' was by William Campbell who worked in London. 'Lieut Colonel David Stewart's Strathspey' is attributed to Niel Gow himself. 'Colonel David Stewart of Garth's Reel' was written by Duncan MacKerchar, also from Inver, who published three collections of music. 'General Stewart of Garth's Reel' was by John and Andrew Gow, sons of Niel. Nor were the Stewart sisters neglected – 'Miss Jessie Stewart of Garth's Reel', 'Miss Stewart of Garth's Reel', 'Miss Stewart of Garth's Strathspey', 'Miss Clementina Stewart's Reel'. Malcolm McDonald even produced 'Drumcharry House'.[171]

In the eyes of young Joseph Mitchell, the dear old colonel may have been chuckling his benign way towards senility but David was only in his early 50s and, as far as he was concerned, in his prime. To repair the old military road, he organised backing from the other heritors and secured a £5,000 loan from the bank. He provided the business plan: 'the number of cattle and sheep which pass through the Drumochter Toll Bar, all of which by Tummel and Tay bridges, and by other traffic, the receipt at these gates from the Garry to the Tay may with certainty be called £400 a year. Indeed the bar at Weem will draw £200 at least. With this sum £200 will be left for repairs and occasional alterations after the £200 for the interest of the £5,000 is paid'.[169] Afterwards he wrote to a friend with pride, describing the road as now being like 'a grand walk from Dalnacardoch to Crieff – all say that were it not for me, it would remain as was as rough as the channel of a burn – next year we will have a stage coach from Crieff to Tummel Bridge to Dalnacardoch'.[172]

With the trunk road being sorted out, he turned his attention to the local highways and almost lost his way amid the unaccustomed shoals of local politics. There was a choice of two routes for the half-dozen miles between Aberfeldy and Kenmore, passing north or south of the Tay, each within sight of the Earl of Breadalbane's splendid seat Taymouth Castle. To the south the road had never been properly reinstated since his lordship had cleared away the tenant farmers round the castle and walled in his enlarged parkland. North of the Tay the bridge across the Lyon at Comrie had been allowed to collapse and traffic was further discouraged since no ferry had replaced it. Sir Neil Menzies, the usual chairman of the half-yearly district road meeting at Weem, was absent so David presided. The local lairds voted to inspect the problem and recommend a remedy. Since Breadalbane's factor was a dissenting voice the meeting adjourned until His Lordship should be available to attend in person.

The colonel then went on his travels in the north of Scotland. When he returned he discovered that the second meeting had been held, at which he had been personally attacked. He had not been selected for the committee charged with carrying out an inspection of the problem and at the previous meeting was accused of having acted in a manner 'unjustifiable and unfounded' and 'accused of personal hostility to the noble earl'.

Directed at Sir Neil Menzies, Stewart's rebuttal takes the form of a 10,000 word memorandum.[173] He briefly discusses the original meeting, then gives his credentials on the subject by rolling out a careful history of the roads round Taymouth. He is in full footnote mode, discoursing, amongst other subjects, on the drinking habits of the early Highlander and the nature of the oaths of allegiance demanded after the '45.

Then he discusses the District Meeting. 'We believed that we were acting for the good of the public ... we believed as honourable men we gave an honest and conscientious opinion ... I was told that we were accused of personal hostility to the Noble Earl ... in short, that the whole was a conspiracy, preconcerted and planned. These are heavy charges ... For my own part I am not in the habit of either forming or joining in conspiracies, nor am I aware that I ever did conduct myself with a malignant mean spirit towards any individual'.

If Lord Breadalbane had bothered to attend more than the two meetings in twenty years at which he has been present, he would know how kindly disposed his neighbours were towards him. It is not I, said Stewart, who states that the roads are poor, but Mr Mitchell, the surveyor of the parliamentary roads. 'However much I respect Lord Breadalbane, however much I wish to forward the improvements and embellishments of his parks, of which, I have said, I am proud, as an honour and ornament to my native glens and mountains; yet all these feelings, however kindly they may be excited, do not carry me to the length of forgetting my duty to my poorer Countrymen, whose character, conduct, and principles deserve better treatment than leaving them to the risk of being drowned in the floods'.

There was a further meeting. Breadalbane and his son Lord Glenorchy were still in a huff with David so the latter, through an intermediary, put forward what he considered the best plan for improvement of the road system. Breadalbane agreed. The motion was put before the meeting. The Noble Lord would 'make such alterations as he might think necessary'. Stewart wanted the alterations to be for 'the best for the public'. The meeting paused. Through his intermediary David received private assurances from the Earl that best for the public will indeed be the criterion selected. The meeting resumed. Glenorchy said no compromise to the original motion. David again halted the meeting until 'Lord Breadalbane says, pay no attention to my son, he is only an individual. I am proprietor of these grounds and I now repeat, that I will execute the improvements you require'.

Breadalbane was second only to Atholl in power locally, and it appears that heritors were pandering to his desires. It also appears that Stewart was the only man with the courage to stand against him and, typically, made extremely sure that his courage was well recognised and that he was right.

A few weeks later he received a letter from William Stewart of Ardvorlich, an influential proprietor from Loch Earn, south-west of Atholl, and the leader of the Strathfillan Society which was one of the organised bodies of Highlanders during the Jaunt. 'My son Robert gave me after his return from Perth the history of your transactions with your neighbours. It was only natural for you to be if possible a peacemaker between them but it often happens that in a case of that kind a man meets with the ill will of both parties ... Glenorchy, by Robt's account, was very insolent'.[174]

An anecdote, recorded by the Fortingall schoolmaster Duncan Campbell, survives from this time which involves Duncan the Piper. The simpleton was employed by the colonel as a messenger between himself and Sir Neil Menzies. Stewart bet Menzies that Duncan's trustworthiness was absolute and that he would not deviate one iota from his instructions. A test was devised. Duncan was given a closed basket with mysterious contents which he was told to deliver, unopened, to Castle Menzies.

The day was hot and Duncan took a rest half way. The basket twitched. Forgetting his promise, Duncan took a peek. Its contents were a letter and a live hare which jumped out and disappeared amid the heather. Duncan took the basket to Sir Neil. 'The latter, having looked at the empty basket, read the note and said "Duncan, in this letter there is a hare –" He was not allowed to finish his sentence. Duncan, cutting a caper, cried in huge delight, "Dilliman! Dilliman! She has got into the letter though she jumped out and ran away when I opened the basket."'[175]

The road question was still rumbling in the spring of 1824 when Sir Neil and Lord Glenorchy called at Drumcharry to find Stewart not at home. 'You will be surprised that I knew not you had called here,' writes the colonel, 'or even that you had been in this part of the country till yesterday – the stupid woman at the gate told me that two lads were asking for me but would not state their names or their business – even this information was not till the day after, and as I could have no idea who it was I thought no more of them. I am exceedingly vexed at this mistake as I was very anxious to see you.

'The woman knew quite well that I had only gone to call on

Cap R Strowan at Duneaves, and that if she had sent me notice I would have been with you in fifteen minutes – You and I perfectly agree in an anxious desire that the question should be settled in the county without going to the County, which would end in an exposure to both Parties – there are busy people (incendiaries I ought to call them) on both sides, stirring up and keeping live a spirit of contention, hostility and opposition.

'In the course of my professional duties I have had considerable experience of such feuds, and by acting impartially and joining no party except that which I conceive to be in the right, I have generally had more information of both sides of a question than others who took a more active lead – Now in the case in question I thought Lord B in the wrong in ... encumbering the public for 25 years with one of the worst pieces of road in the County except sometimes in the old military road, and this within his Parks and Pleasure Grounds ... I thought the thing ought to be altered – and voted accordingly – but when I found that Lord B had consented to improve the road and accommodate the Public I supported him, and opposed those who would not accept of his pledge and who voted against him right or wrong'.[176]

As one might expect, David was involved with the local Highland Societies. In the summer of 1824 came the foundation of the Association of Atholemen. For centuries the Stewarts and Robertsons of Atholl had fought alongside each other and interbred. David Stewart and Captain Robertson of Struan (Strowan), resident at Duneaves over the Lyon from Drumcharry and new chief of Clan Donnachaidh, summoned a meeting of the gentry of the two names 'for the purpose of promoting and cementing a generous, manly, and Brotherly friendship between the two Clans, such as subsisted between their ancestors, also to revive and cherish a proper Highland spirit and feeling among the members of the two Clans, and give encouragement to every species of industry, for which this part of the Country is well adapted, and especially the manufacture at home and the general adoption of dress of those fabricks which have ever been peculiar to the Highlands, namely Tartans, Plaids, and Bonnets'.[177]

One result of this was the Highland games at Bridge of Tilt, much disapproved by His Grace of Atholl for the hooliganism and drunkenness that sometimes prevailed there. These survive as the Atholl Highland Games. Another result was a link formed in 1996 between the two kindred to promote a joint museum at Bruar. But Stewart's summer as a country gentleman was blighted by a tragedy.

CHAPTER TWENTY

Jobs and Money

'Yet not a word of a will or of money'

Hanging over everything Stewart was doing were, of course, his debts. Since taking over the management of the family lands in 1820, he had been using Alexander Irvine as a sounding board for all the schemes for improvement on the estate and kept him informed about all the financial shufflings that had to be carried out. Irvine was left in charge when the laird went to London or Edinburgh and, even when he was at Drumcharry, letters winged between there and the manse at Little Dunkeld.

In the summer of 1824 they were building a lime kiln close to Drumcharry, and discussing how best to take advantage of a reduction in interest rates. At one stage 5% had to be paid to creditors; now the Perth Bank was paying investors 2.5% and Stewart was hoping to reduce his interest payments to 3%. Then a black-edged missive arrived.

'Dr Irvine died here this morning at 6 o'clock. Little Dunkeld 31st July 1824.' Immediately after talking to the pupils of the grammar school the previous afternoon, the minister, aged 52 – the same as David – suffered a stroke. He was carried back to the manse where he had died. His obituary in the *Perthshire Courier* described him as a profound Celtic and Oriental scholar, one of the compilers of the *Gaelic Dictionary* produced by the Highland Society of Scotland and the donor to the Highland Society of London of a large body of Celtic poetry which he had collected in the Highlands and Islands at oral recitations. This collection is now lodged in the National Library of Scotland in Edinburgh.[178] He had also revised the Gaelic Bible for publication by the Society for Propagating Christian Knowledge and had been a keen promoter of Gaelic schools. His obituary said that 'he was endeared by a warm generosity of temper, and an unaffected kindness of manner, that are seldom combined, to an equal extent, in the same individual.'

The funeral was held on 3rd August and his widow erected a set of iron railings round his grave at a cost of £27 19s 6d to discourage resurrectionists and paid another £1 10s to have them painted. Stewart had lost a lifelong friend, a disciple, and an adviser. He had also gained a family. The manse was needed for the new minister so Jessie moved to Drumcharry to live with her elder sister and brother. She brought her children with her. Sandy, the oldest, was 17 and had obtained a foundation bursary at St Andrews University. Clementina, her second, was 15. Robert was 14, David 13, William 11, and James John 8. Three of her boys had been at school in Dunkeld; the youngest, James John, was sickly and barely survived to adulthood. Jessie also had a niece and a nephew in her entourage. The niece was Grenada-born Ann, now a year in Scotland. The nephew was Neil, the colonel's own motherless byblow.

'I had a sister of mine married about 20 years ago, a man with more learning in his head than money in his pocket,' wrote Stewart to an acquaintance, 'and when he died left four sons with little means for their education & support. I therefore have taken them in charge but, with a family estate overwhelmed with debt, I cannot do what I wish and must in consequence encroach on the indulgences of friends.' [179] There were actually five sons but he was probably discounting the youngest whose health marked him out for an early death.

The estates were populated by lots of Irvine relations but David had the responsibility of ensuring that his nephews consolidated their father's climb to the ranks of the professional and mercantile classes. For his namesake David, perhaps the pick of the bunch, he found a job in a merchant's house in Glasgow from where he supplied the family sugar plantation in Trinidad. Robert went to the island to work with his uncle John. William studied medicine in Glasgow. Clementina would wed cousin Charles from Bohally across the Tummel from Kynachan.

Sandy was 17 when his father died and was studying divinity at St Andrews. Notwithstanding his youth 'a group of elders of lower order' lobbied the Duke of Atholl with a petition asking him to appoint the young man to Little Dunkeld in succession to his father. Jessie was involved in this too, her excuse being that Dr Irvine's successor was unsuitable because he had no Gaelic, a failure in the Highland clergy which David Stewart had pinpointed in the *Sketches*.[180]

Unsurprisingly, Sandy Irvine was considered too young for the post but his Uncle David was working towards creating a job for him at Foss. Dr Chalmers, a friend of Alexander Irvine and a prominent churchman, had lobbied the government through the General Assembly to build 40 new churches and manses in remote areas of the Highlands.

Fortingall was the largest parish in all Scotland, stretching into Glen Lyon, over to Strathtummel, and had its boundaries at the headwaters of the Tay on Rannoch Moor. Kinloch Rannoch had a resident missionary – Alexander Irvine held the post in 1799. Foss and Glen Lyon each had only a preaching station where an itinerant minister would hold an occasional service. Stewart decided to improve the situation. 'I am fighting hard for the new churches and ministers with £120 stipend for Glenlyon and Foss – none of the proprietors give themselves any trouble – the Rannoch people are trying for Kinloch, but as usual they disagree, and will not get a minister'.[181]

Foss with its ruined church on the edge of the Kynachan estate was earmarked for young Sandy. His Gaelic was considered 'rather clipped' and he took his time about completing his examinations but his uncle wrote, 'When I heard the probable delay in his Trials, I got the settlement of the minister of Foss postponed for another year – he must be ready then – it is no small matter to get two ministers and stipends when great men have been refused'.

In a later letter David says to 'remind Alex that he should have testimonials ready for the Presbytery of Dunkeld – from the Professors whose classes he attended – from Principals Baird and

Haldane incidentally – all testifying to his qualifications for a church in the Highlands – with consequently a full knowledge of the Gaelic language ... I will enclose them along with a letter of application and recommendation to the Secretary of State for the Church of Foss which I suppose will be ready next summer ... I am in good favour with the Commissioners at present and as I have given two and a half acres of good land to the minister and have otherwise pleased them with my manner of proceeding, I have reason to hope that they will pay all the expense of the Church repairs, but this cannot be settled for some time and I must act as if I think I will have to pay all – The Commissioners pay me the compliment to say that if it were not for me, they would not grant a church a stipend in Perthshire, so Foss, Glenlyon, Rannoch may thank me for their being parishes. – I wish I could succeed so well for myself – but I see no prospect of that'.[182]

In May 1825 David, filling the shoes of dead half-pay officers, was promoted to major-general, which brought him a useful increase in income but little else. He was soon down in London once more doing his rounds in search of an appointment. With her husband dead it was Jessie who looked after the management of Drumcharry in his absence. She became the recipient of his colourful letters and heard about his attempts to find money. He was staying in Chelsea with his father's doddery cousin, Alexander Stewart, retired colonel-surgeon of the 73rd Regiment, who was the correspondent who had advised the colonel to go for Dr Robertson's deep cutting technique when his wound had flared up in early 1816.

'I see Dr Stewart very often,' wrote the new general. 'To tell you the truth to keep near him, to keep me in his eye, and to keep improper people at a distance, is the principal cause of my remaining in London so long – I believe no person stands so well in his opinion as I do – indeed he often tells me so and the tears run down his cheeks when he speaks and cries out – "I am proud of you, I am proud of being of the family of which you are the head and which you have brought so much into the notice of the world, and made the name of Garth known to thousands – to millions – Royalty makes companions of you – you have the best qualities of your father mixed with your mother's character, and no woman who ever lived I esteemed and respected so much as I did her." These are strong expressions and often repeated but yet not a word of a will or of money – yet I must see him frequently and not lose sight of him – Not later than yesterday he pointed out in the last quarterly Review a note of very high approbation of my Book and as usual tears so filled his eyes that he could not see to read ... Dr Stewart now comes downstairs, and altho' much failed, has no complaint but weakness – his mind strong and alive as ever'.[181]

Dr Stewart was descended from the tacksman of a farm in Glencoe called Achnacone. This man, Duncan, was probably a younger son of the 5th laird of Achnacone in Appin and had been sent to Glencoe after the Massacre in 1692 by the chief of the Appin Stewarts, Ardsheal, to guard the flank of the clan's territory. Duncan's son had married *Fear Ghart*'s aunt in 1747 and the doctor was their only child. He had never married, his mistress was already dead and somehow he had amassed a very respectable sum of money.

David could not wait in London until Dr Stewart died but he returned north with the knowledge that he had been appointed an executor of the will. At the end of November 1826 a great blizzard swept across the Highlands. For two days the storm raged and when it had blown itself out, the country was blanketed in snowdrifts up to 20 feet deep. Six lives are known to have been lost in Atholl, most of them watchers over livestock in the hills. Both cattle and sheep were buried beneath the snow and the whole population was mobilised to dig them out. So deep were some of the drifts that the sides of holes dug towards the trapped beasts needed to be shored to prevent collapse, and men stood by to rescue the rescuers should they be buried beneath a cave-in. In Atholl, great numbers of trees were blown down, 10,000 sheep and scores of cattle were lost. Frantic efforts were made to preserve the carcasses and dead sheep were sold off at seventeen shillings a couple.[183]

It was fortunate that the storm occurred at the beginning of winter rather than the end when stores would have been depleted but the cost was borne by tenants and lairds alike. When a farmer lost his stock he could not pay rent and thus shared losses with his landlord. David was chieftain at the Atholl Gathering of 1827, a gloomy time for him since interest payments take no account of natural disasters but 1828 was better and it began with two deaths. The first was that of Glengarry. He was on board the *Stirling* steamship when it ran aground in Loch Linnhe; he jumped overboard, slipped, and fell on his head on a rock. It is unlikely that David mourned. The second was that of Dr Stewart.

The good doctor left £18,000 in the 3% Consolidated Fund.[184] £2,000 was bequeathed to indigent cousins who raised a clamour of disappointment; £3,000 was left to a rich kinsman, Alexander Macdonald of Moy; £5,000 went to old army comrades; £3,000 went as bursaries to St Andrews University and, praise be, £5,000 came to David. As chief executor, he had to sort out the bursaries. They came to be called the Garth Bursaries; six were awarded annually; the head of the Garth family would hold the patronage of three. And so it remained until the representative of the Garth Stewarts assigned them to the University Court in 1975. There are indications that David did not intend to take posterity's admiration for his cousin's generosity entirely unto himself, but his mind was occupied with matters far more interesting than ensuring they were called after Achnacone. He was at last offered a job.

CHAPTER TWENTY-ONE

Governor of St Lucia

'When his Royal Highness is King, I think he will be my friend'

IN THE SUMMER of 1828 Stewart's perseverance at last paid off. At the age of 56 he was appointed Governor and Military Commander of St Lucia. Pausing only to pack his trunks and split the business of the estate between an Edinburgh WS, Robert Rattray, and Jessie he caught the mail coach to London and took rooms in Parliament Street to prepare himself for the task in hand.

The position was no plum. The island was one of the most dangerous places on earth – hot, jungly, humid, teeming with poisonous snakes and fetid, disease-ridden swamps. In 1789 the French Revolution had turned St Lucian society upside down. Priests fled and churches were burned. Slaves were killed, joined bands of brigands, or died from disease or starvation. The island was fought over several times. In the eleven-month campaign against the French from June 1796 Sir Ralph Abercromby lost 78% of the troops under his command. The economy had been ruined by warfare and further devastated by hurricanes in 1817 and 1819, the last of which had killed the Governor. Since 1790 the white population had declined by 65%. But David was one of the survivors of Sir Ralph's campaign. He knew the country and, where others might fear for his health and his life, he was blithely confident about the strength of his constitution.

One of his first actions after arriving in London was to spend some of Dr Stewart's money on silver; he ordered a large rectangular salver with four legs and two handles, an egg-cup stand with six egg-cups and six spoons, and a set of cutlery. All of these were engraved with the crests of Garth and Kynachan enclosed within a strap bearing the family motto 'Beware', again with his Order of the Bath dangling below. Investing in bullion was a good way of preserving capital, and the obvious thought is that he may have intended his silver to make an impressive show for visitors to Government House. Most probably his main feeling was that it was right and proper for a man of his rank and with his background to have his own plate, just as his ancestors had had theirs.

In the euphoria of the moment he also wrote an account of the Battle of Maida and sent it to Sir George Murray, the Colonial Secretary, asking him to recommend it to King Ferdinand of the Two Sicilies in the hope that His Majesty would award a medal to the surviving officers, Stewart and Glengarry's younger brother. The latter had joined the 78th as a major on the same day as David; he was now a hero of Waterloo and a retired Lieutenant-Colonel of the Coldstream Guards.[46] Murray drily advised that it was customary for the donor to make the approach, not an aspiring recipient.

David next set out to discover what his authority and duties in St Lucia would be.[185] The island and most of its whites had been French. Were the laws of France or England applied? Was the final say in the Supreme Court the prerogative of the President or a majority of the judges? Was there a right of appeal to the Governor? Could he commute a death sentence? Was the Privy Council at which the Governor presided a legislative council or merely advisory? Who appointed the Privy Councillors? Could the Governor replace ineffective or corrupt members? Could he overrule the Council?

He also asked for any additional information 'as will contribute to enable him to accomplish the object he has in view which is by an honourable and zealous discharge of his duty – by unremitting attention, by a fine, determined, but at the same time mild line of conduct, doing justice to all, supporting those who deserve encouragement, but checking those whose conduct is the reverse – By these means and having already considerable knowledge of the West Indies, of the inhabitants, and of the country in general, I hope to be able to carry on the duties of my situation to the satisfaction of His Majesty and of his Government to the happiness and comfort of the people and the prosperity of the country in general'.

The new Governor wrote to tell Sir Walter Scott of his good fortune, complimenting the author on the recently published *Fair Maid of Perth* and concluded: 'Several lady friends of mine are most anxious to possess your signature. Will you favour me with a few lines and multiply your signature as often as the paper will hold?' [186]

Sir Walter returned a sweet letter of au revoir to his old friend. 'I rejoice in your appointment since it holds out to you the means of obtaining some of the good things of fortune which cannot be lodged in kinder or more generous hands. I am quite sure that men of all colours and connections will find in you a paternal ruler ... I look forward with greater pleasure to hailing you once more among high bonnets and brave fellows with the Nish, Nish, Nish I have so often joined you in ... And now my dear general, to know that you have the power of doing good is to know that you are well and happy'.[187] And, bless him, the Laird of Abbotsford did the autographing: 'I send a list of subscriptions on the other side. It is vain in me perhaps even to comply with a request so flattering, but you ask it, and whether in joke or earnest your request must be obeyed'. The letter ends with what Scott admits is a ghastly piece of doggerel:

1. Brave Stuart, name without a blot
   Yours to command is Walter Scott
2. Whate'er in Waverley is wrote
   I bear the blame, quoth Walter Scott
3. A grey auld man, sair failed I wot
   There's life in't yet, said Walter Scott
4. Trees did he plant and lands he bought
   A Darnick laird was Walter Scott
5. He loved a man that bravely fought
   And Garth was friend to Walter Scott

6   With Highland Chiefs he had a vote
    For well the plaids loved Walter Scott
7   His greyhounds good were fleet as thought
    Till age tamed them and Walter Scott
8   Call this vile stuff, I reck it not
    So there's an end to Walter Scott

Pray dont let the papers get this off-hand nonsense, and now adieu once more and up with the bonny blue bonnet. The dirk and the feather, etc'.

The 'nishing' was part of the after-dinner toast known as the Highland Honours. The company arose. Each member placed one foot on his chair, the other on the table, exclaimed 'Nish, nish, shouter-a-nish, a-ris, a-ris, a-ris!', brandished his glass, drained it, and hurled it into the fireplace. This last part was often omitted, particularly if ladies were present when one also had to take care with the arrangement of one's kilt.

Memoranda were now blizzarding the Colonial Office with recommendations and appointments. It was a particularly delicate time in the West Indies because the economy depended upon slavery, and the run-up to emancipation in 1834 had begun. From this time survives a prayer in Stewart's most hurried and perfunctory script – the only indication of his beliefs and perhaps a sign of where he thought his own weaknesses of character might lie.

'Lord thou knowest the weakness and corruption of my nature, and the manifold temptations I daily mend with, I therefore humbly beseech thee to have compassion upon my infirmities and to give me the constant assistance of thy grace and holy spirit that I may be restrained from sin, and adhere to my duty ... Grant me patience under any affliction thou shall see fit to lay upon me, and my mind always contented with my present condition ... Purge my heart from every hatred and malice and that I may always go to rest in peace with a conscience void of offence towards thee, and towards all men ... Oh let not sickness or death come upon me unawares, or find me in a state unprepared ... teach and instruct me that I may manage those affairs which are now derived upon me with prudence, justice, and integrity. Let not my carriage and behaviour, O Lord, be vain and fantastic, light and foolish, but decent and modest and suitable to this condition thou hast been pleased to bring me to ... and grant O Lord that I may always prefer the firmness and honesty of mind to adhere without fear to the path I believe to be agreeable to thy word – may no regard to the opinions of mankind ever make me betray my own conscience ... Above all grant O heavenly Father, that the truths of thy word may have a practical effect upon my temper and conduct ... enable me to form a correct estimate of my situation in life, and of the duty to which this situation calls me – and thus may I be enabled by thy grace to acquit myself in all things as a good servant of my Father who is in Heaven'.[188]

As well as worrying about the new job Stewart was also worrying about the responsibilities he had dumped on Jessie back home – and he was being badgered by the Duke of Clarence who wanted him to preside at one of those Scotch dinners where much nish-nishing would take place. It was well worth telling his sister about this last in a long letter, full of final instructions, which he sent at the beginning of December.

'The Duke of Clarence kept me from 1 o'clock till near 3 the last day I called at Bushy Park – he was most gracious – paid me marked attention and talked on very confidential subjects – He takes a warm interest in the West Indies and is a good friend to the Planters. He asked about my brothers and sisters – I told him what had been done and what was intended to be done for your boys – He approves highly of the West Indies plans – one part of his words was "You have acted like a man of judgment and independent mind – you will place your orphan nephews in situations where they will have the power of making themselves independent and this you have done without asking favours or depending on others."

'Thus you see, my dear Jessie, how feelingly he speaks of familiar and family subjects. He was ten years in the West Indies and knows the country well – He pays me a high compliment in desiring me to take the chair at the St Andrews Dinner in his absence – the thing is too much for me, and I have applied and begged Lord Roseberry to take the duty – When his Royal Highness is King, I think he will be my friend'.[182]

In an engaging juxtaposition, David changes the subject to more mundane concerns. 'Be sure to write to me regularly – I send you a supply of paper for yourself and for the boys, and some to be laid aside for myself till my return – Altho the paper appears fine it is as cheap as all things I purchase. The Paper is only eleven pence the quire of 40 sheets – there are some damaged leaves but considering the price not many. The cloaks I send to you and your sister cost only £1–2 each – yours only one pound and the other 22 shillings. The bonnet for John McPherson's wife only 4/– and 2/– for the ribbons. Don't tell her this as she will think the less of them – The broad ribbons for the girls are only seven pence the yard – the narrow four pence – Read the Perth Courier as usual and put Government House St Lucia, and return to the Post office and Kippen will charge me with three halfpence postage for each paper which D Campbell will pay with my other postages'.

By 8th December the general was at Falmouth scribbling a final letter to a friend before he embarked for the West Indies. In it he gives a neat summation of his attitude to life. 'An attempt to do my best in all things I did – all things I ought to do and all things I attempt to do – and to do to others as I would be done by'.[189]

CHAPTER TWENTY-TWO

The Dying Days of Slavery

'The next point of which Planters complain is depriving the overseers and drivers of their badge of office – the cat or whip'

THE PASSAGE took five weeks and David landed on St Lucia on 17th January 1829. He had brought with him a personal secretary, J. D. Blythe, but no military ADC since he was not on the general staff. Government House, high on the hill south of the shabby little capital of Castries, was without servants. The garden and surrounding ground was untilled and, although the rainy season was past, noxious smells still rose up the slope from the great rotting swamp adjacent to the town beneath. It must have been forcibly brought home to the new Governor just what a backwater his post was. Behind and above the house was the fortress of Morne Fortune. Thirty years earlier he had been part of the bloody assault upon the French who then commanded it.

The new Governor's first dispatch home was full of optimism; he was gathering local knowledge, had found the law – particularly new regulations regarding the treatment of slaves – obeyed, and the natural riches of the island were such that it should become a jewel in His Majesty's crown.[190] In a private letter to Sir George Murray, David is less sanguine, asking for representations on his behalf at Horse Guards for a job in military government somewhere else. Sir George held out little hope. There were many candidates for such posts; meantime the Governor should stay healthy and manage his government without squabbles amongst his officials.[191]

Clementina died that spring, the news reaching the West Indies in May. Her brother sent comfort home to Jessie. 'Always ready to do good – ever anxious to assist the sick and the distressed, and to promote the comfort and happiness of all around – all that came within her circle – if such qualifications meet with everlasting reward, who had a better claim than our sister ... Poor Clementina died in the same room and in the same house in which she had passed so many happy years and slept so many nights, with a conscience clear of all blame or self reproach'.[192]

In a private letter to Murray, Stewart explained the methods he intended to follow in governing the colony. Sir George approved: 'I am quite disposed to concur in the view you seem to take, of its being greatly better to persuade, and to guide gently, and by example, when that is practicable, than to urge persons towards that which is right and for their own ultimate advantage. And this is most expressly the case when an undertaking of so difficult and delicate a nature is going forward as that of altering the system of society and gradually introducing freedom where slavery has long prevailed. You act judiciously also in not proposing too much in the way of improvement, but in getting something done'.[193]

Riding round the island, seeming to poke his nose into every hut, David was employing his well-tried system of gathering all the facts he could before coming to conclusions and initiating action. Not until July was he ready to give London a detailed description of the condition of the slaves and his recommendations for improvement. By then the rumours that sailed across from the West Indies aboard every ship had him twice dead with fever and once married. He was attacked by a severe bout of illness at the height of the rainy season. His letter to Sir George on the subject is characteristically insouciant.

'Near a fortnight ago a kind of flying fever or influenza came across this establishment and attacked white, black and coloured – Seven servants sick at once – I was the last attacked and the first recovered – Availing myself of former experience and having a constitution capable of withstanding any medicine, I undermined and took the fever by storm – By ample doses and stewing myself to the consistence of a scalded calf's head by perspiration, I overcame the fever in twenty seven hours – A few days care restored my strength and I am as well as ever – I hope I have given a lesson to our medical men – I did not interfere with their treatment of the servants – none are recovered but all out of danger'.[194]

He was now ready to make changes. Troops stationed on Pigeon Island, a barren rock north of the capital, were healthy. Those at Morne Fortune up behind Government House were not. The cause, suggested David, was the adjacent jungle and swamp. He requested permission to spend £500 removing the trees and draining the morass. 'A noxious vapour is emitted from this mass of corruption, and strikes at the first blow direct into the Barrack windows,' causing 'inflammatory fevers, agues, and consequent general debility, and decay of all the powers of the body'.[195] The forest brought another problem 'both dangerous and disgusting' by sheltering 'numbers of venomous serpents which were seen crawling about the Garrison every morning'. When drained, the swamp would provide an excellent parade ground for the soldiers.

'Poverty,' replied Sir George with the cry of the bureaucrat down the ages. 'It seems at present to be the prevailing malady, and in this Climate as well as with you, it has attacked both the Public and Individuals'. The Governor could not spend more than £100 without reference to London.

So be it, responded David, and he then outlined the state of decay into which the island had fallen. But he was not sitting still. Since the Colonial Office would not provide the necessary cash, he was busy raising it locally. He was expecting to top £4,000 for rebuilding a Protestant and a Catholic church. More than a £1,000 was being spent on a new wharf at Castries. The road adjacent was being built on a reclaimed swamp, its cost to be met by selling off the drained land for building plots. He had persuaded planters to assign slaves to begin repairs to the devasted road system. From an iron foundry in Edinburgh, he had ordered four precast bridges and water pipes to make redundant a 22-mile boat trip to bring water to the capital. He had also commissioned iron railings to make the jail secure.[196]

David's magnum opus was sent in September. This was his report on the condition of the slaves. He was an expert, reminding

Whitehall again that he had studied the problems of slavery in 1796–7 when the Africa trade was still operating, and then for five years from 1808. Since arriving in St Lucia he had made 'a minute inspection which, believe me, surprised many at seeing me take so much personal trouble and fatigue,'[197] during which he had examined virtually every plantation on the island.

In general the slaves were contented. They were well nourished thanks to the fertility of the soil and they had their own allotments from which they could sell produce and eventually buy their freedom should they so wish. The women dressed well and visitors were surprised to see 'forty, fifty or a greater number of women working in the fields with hoes or other implements and dressed in white or printed calico jackets and Petticoats'. They worked proper hours and the old and sick were cared for in hospitals.

Thirty-nine plantations were satisfactory – 17 less so because of heavy debt. At peak times some of the latter worked their slaves late into the night and, although the Negroes were allowed the following day off, this was a practice Stewart would stop. Even the slaves on the poorest estates had some security. Before creditors saw a penny, the needs of the slaves had first call on an estate's produce. Some slaves 'would sell their own father or child for a cask of rum'. They needed schools, but required moral education as much as 'the mechanical art of reading'.

The new slave laws were working well in most instances but female transgressors could now delay punishment through the appeals procedure and were impervious to any discipline during this hiatus. 'While women are sent to the treadmill and whipped in England, it is carrying philanthropy to its full extent to prevent an application of similar checks to females of other countries'. (The mill was not forbidden, some colonial office functionary noted in the report's margin.)

To cool tempers, no slave could be punished within 24 hours of the transgression. His own experience in controlling the incorrigibles of the Royal West India Rangers, said David, proved that swift and, if necessary, harsh punishments had a wonderful effect on behaviour.

'The next point of which Planters complain is depriving the overseers and drivers of their badge of office – the cat or whip. This is only objectionable as being perhaps too suddenly done. So revolting to the feelings as a practice must be of keeping people to their work by compulsion and fear of punishment, <u>it cannot be too soon removed</u>. But in so doing great caution is requested as with the fiery stubborn dispositions of many Negroes, the fear of immediate punishment is as necessary as I found it with my culprit soldiers'.

The Governor had just been faced with what amounted to a slave revolt. It had been triggered by the President of the Supreme Court, Mr Jeremie, who had rebuked a harsh overseer in the presence of a hundred slaves. They had taken this to mean that punishments were now suspended and on some estates they had smashed the sugar boilers and mills, and many had taken to the jungle. Stewart's response gives something of the political correctness of the attitude to slavery in the dying years of the institution.

'I commenced by ordering the Protector of Slaves, the King's Proctor & Procurator Fiscal, and the Commandant or Justice of Peace of the Quarter to repair to the plantation where the slaves were most unruly and rebellious; and to make the strictest inquiry into all the circumstances; and to report to me if any of the slaves appeared in fault, but not to punish till they heard from me; and if the proprietor or his white servants were to blame, to send them by warrant to jail. On this examination it was found that the proprietors' conduct was quite correct and that the poor people were deceived by false reports and led to believe that the king had made them free'.

David punished nobody, but sent the militia and every soldier on the island into the jungle with instructions to go to the places where the slaves might be hiding, fire blanks, and make such a hullabaloo that the fugitives would be convinced that their only place of safety would be back home. Within a fortnight not only had every runaway returned to the plantations but 'one slave came in who had been 16 years in the mountains'.

The report ends with a case which again illuminates the transformation of the rights of the slaves. On one of the more dilapidated estates, the owner's son-in-law, M. Dominique Drivon, was before the courts accused by his slaves of providing inadequate clothing, 'working the negroes beyond their strength, refusing the usual interval of rest, and the time for cultivating their own lots of land, and at the same time stinting the quantity of salt fish or beef usually allowed'. Stewart instructed the Protector of Slaves to supply clothing against the owner's credit and then let the law take its course to see how it would operate.

Drivon was fined $400 and banned from the plantation. He appealed and the sentence was changed to a fine of $450 but the ban was lifted. He appealed again to the Royal Court and the decision was deferred for two months. Stewart was not impressed with the law's delays. He writes that he should have followed his first instinct and removed the accused from the estate. ('By what authority?' asks the margin.)

Written from Pigeon Island to which he had retired for the sake of his health after his attack of fever in July, this was to be the last of David's reports. In the middle of November he returned to Government House and, on the 30th, he hosted his big St Andrew's Night party. He was in cracking form, appearing 'in the Highland costume and was very happy'. A few days later he fell ill with the fever that killed him.

CHAPTER TWENTY-THREE

Aftermath

'He was covered with golden opinions by all ranks and classes'

THE SENIOR MILITARY officer on St Lucia, Captain Delhoot of the 35th, took over the administration of government. His dispatch announcing David's death did not arrive in London until 11th February 1830.

Meantime the St Lucians donned their mourning, dancing and celebrations were discontinued and the shops of the capital were shut for the day of the funeral. The body was embalmed and placed in a lead coffin so that it could be repatriated for burial beneath the ancient yew in Fortingall should the family so wish. Meantime it was interred in the shade of a grove of trees in Morne Fortune military cemetery in a little governor's corner where it still lies. Around are buried some 200 other soldiers with whom he fought on this spot. He is one of a handful of men of the 42nd, struck down more than thirty years after the battle which cost the lives of the others.

The front page of the weekly *L'Impartial* – published, nevertheless, by the government – was wholly taken up with an elegy to the general – in one column the English version and in the other the rather more elegant French. Sir James Lyon, Governor of the Windward Islands, had chartered a ship to carry the Doctor Inspector of Hospitals across to St Lucia as soon as news of the illness was known. Now the vessel went on to Trinidad to return with John Stewart.

He wrote a sad letter back to Jessie. 'Our beloved brother's loss will not only be sorely felt by us, but by the inhabitants of the Island, as they observe themselves, they lose in him a father, a friend who was devoted to their interest and I much fear my dear sister that his anxiety for that unfortunate colony hurried his death ... The death of our worthy father and Brother William I must confess, did not affect me so much as the sudden death of David'.[199]

In its obituary *The Gentleman's Magazine* summed up David's career, praised the *Sketches*, and added: 'In every relation of life Gen Stewart was highly esteemed;- a brave and gallant soldier, a patriotic and warm lover of his country, he was known to a very wide circle in society; and whether as the officer, the citizen, the Scotsman, or the man, he was covered with golden opinions by all ranks and classes. It was only about twelve months ago, with all the spirit and gaiety of a youthful veteran, he sailed for St Lucia, to the government of which he was appointed; he jested of his return and marriage at the end of a few years'.[200]

John became head of the family of Drumcharry, Garth, Inchgarth, and Kynachan but he did not return home before his death in 1832. His sugar estate passed to Jessie and, under the management of local agents, stayed in the family, yielding very little until it was sold in the 1840s. Robert Irvine, the second of Jessie's sons, who had joined his uncle in Trinidad, died of fever in March 1830 only three months after the general.

Jessie inherited responsibility for the Highland Perthshire estates after David's death but they were unsustainable. The house contents were auctioned. Sir Neil Menzies bought the library – a remarkably tedious collection of volumes consisting largely of army lists, books on Scots law, some classics, and dubious literature from the previous century. Much of the silver went but Jessie managed to buy some family pieces. Kynachan was sold to Sir Neil, and the three other estates were purchased by Sir Archibald Campbell of Ava, representative of the Stewarts' old adversaries the Campbells of Glenlyon, who had been to school in Fortingall with David and was already occupying Drumcharry House as a tenant. He knocked it down and built a grand mansion on the site which he called Garth House. All that remained in the family was the burial plot beneath the old yew tree by Fortingall kirk.

When David took on the estates in 1821, the debt stood at

£40,000. When they were sold, unsecured debts amounted to £19,492. A dividend of 10s in the pound was paid immediately and a further 5s later. Two hundred creditors are listed.[125] The vast majority were country people living in townships from Loch Tayside to Fortingall and Aberfeldy. Forty-six were tenants on the Stewart estates and they were owed sums ranging from £3 to a widow living near the kirktown, to £100 to one of the McDougalls. Christian McLean, mother of David's bastard, put in for more than £200 but her claim was disallowed. Jessie was owed nearly £3,000.

A claim for £122 from Capt. Alex Stewart, Gibraltar, was also disallowed. He was *Fear Ghart*'s illegitimate son and was to turn up in Glasgow in 1837 alarming David Irvine, the third of the four brothers and a merchant who supplied the family sugar estate and marketed its produce.

'I really know nothing of Captain Sandy,' he wrote to his eldest sibling. 'I asked no questions that could lead into any explanation of his intentions in coming to Scotland – neither did I ask after his wife or family ... in short our intercourse was confined to very commonplace attention on my part ... he has many friends here I find, and some correspondence with parties abroad – That is reason enough for me – He may have it in his power to be troublesome, and you know he has little principles to restrain him – He is not in the 94th I have ascertained. Find out where he is & what his intentions are. I dare say Rattray [the Edinburgh WS] & he having been raising Cinders & we would all need to be on our guard'.[118]

David would die of cholera in 1842, contracted whilst doing charity work during an epidemic in the Glasgow slums. William, the fourth of the general's nephews, practised medicine for many years in Pitlochry where he was known as the 'Guid Doctor', always with a sugar almond in his pocket to give to a child. The Irvine Memorial Hospital in the town is a tribute to his impact. Clementina, the only daughter of the Irvine family, married her cousin Charles McDiarmid from Bohally in 1839. Immediately the young couple emigrated to Australia and she died on the voyage.

Sandy, the eldest, was inducted to the new kirk of Foss in 1830 whilst his uncle David's influence lingered and his mother's family were still leading heritors in the parish. All the brothers consolidated their father's ascent to the middle classes but Sandy climbed highest. He married first a daughter of the laird of Foss and, when she died, the only child and heiress of his uncle's old friend Captain Duncan Robertson of Kindrochet. Sandy became minister of Fortingall and later Blair Atholl where he died in the very grand manse in 1867 – a doctor of divinity like his father. Sandy's own minister son briefly became a landed gentleman before the Kindrochet estate was sold to the Duke of Atholl in 1883.

Jessie moved with her niece Ann to a cottage outside Pitlochry. By the time the younger woman died in 1859 they were living in Dr William's large new house on the edge of the town overlooking the river Tummel. The old lady lived on until she was 89, her mind still sharp. A photograph of her in old age shows her in her lace mutch headdress sitting at her spinning wheel in front of her thatched cottage, a figure that could easily have come from the century before. She was the last of the 'kindly Stewarts of Garth'.

Every historian and novelist who writes on the Highlands of the past draws directly or indirectly on David Stewart's work. The most ferocious polemicist against the Clearances, Donald MacLeod from Strathnaver, himself twice dispossessed to make way for sheep and no friend to any laird, described the *Sketches* in one of his 1840 letters to the *Edinburgh Weekly Chronicle* as an 'excellent work to which I beg to call the attention of every friend to truth and justice, and especially those who take an interest in the fate of the expatriated tenantry. The General has completely vindicated the character of the Highland tenantry, and shown the impolicy, as well as the cruelty, of the means used for their ejection'. In another letter, a crunching rebuttal of Harriet Beecher Stowe's *Happy Memories* which sang the praises of Lady Stafford, MacLeod talks of the 'noble-minded, immortal General'. He quotes from the *Sketches* but 'cannot help being grieved by my unavoidable abbreviation of these heart-stirring and heart-warming extracts, which should ornament every mantel-piece and library in the Highlands of Scotland'.[201]

Although J. M. Scrymgeour painted the iconic portrait of David in his Highland garb in 1825, it was not exhibited at the Royal Academy until 1832. The silver sword presented by the officers of the 78th is carefully depicted. This picture was the basis of an engraving by S. R Reynolds, commissioned by Scrymgeour, dedicated to the 'Noblemen and Gentlemen of the Highlands of Scotland and to the Officers of the Highland Regiments' which sold by the score.

The little caricature of David was the frontispiece in the commonplace book of Caroline Norton. Her first entry is an elegy on his death which contains the lines 'The first to dry the mourner's tear, To pity's claims ere lent an ear, How long till thou canst find another, To all a Father, Friend, or Brother. The fairest Gem that falls from Beauty's eye, More precious far than aught which gold can buy, Is due to him, now sunk beneath the pall, A generous foe, the kindest friend, & loved by all'. She was a Sheridan by birth, later a successful novelist 'distinguished for her beauty and wit'. Her brother-in-law, Lord Grantley, had an estate in Rannoch; her sister-in-law was married to Sir Neil Menzies. She spent summers in Highland Perthshire in the 1820s and would have known her subject in life.

The *Sketches* was reprinted twice in David's lifetime, again in 1885. For that edition one newspaper critic wrote: 'Without any doubt Stewart's Sketches is one of the best, if not the very best book, published on the subject. It has formed the groundwork for all the subsequent publications on the Highlands and the Highland Clans ... Sir Walter Scott and General Stewart have done to the Highlanders the justice denied them by others. The magic wand of the one, and the facile pen and intimate knowledge of the other, painted their character and heroism in letters of gold, ineffaceable, imperishable'. The second edition was reprinted by John Donald in 1977. The latest reprint was in 1993 from the Bantam Press.

There were moves afoot to erect a memorial to David Stewart

in the 1880s and these finally came to fruition in 1925. In the presence of an honour guard of the Black Watch and a large group of spectators, the statue, designed by A. S. Gamley R.S.A. and carved from a six-ton block of granite, was unveiled at Keltneyburn by the 8th Duke of Atholl. He made the speech and, since David would have delighted in hearing his praises sung from such a quarter, the last words shall be left to His Grace.

'It was his ardour and pertinacity, and his love for the men of the hills that first made people further south realise the magnificent material to be found in the Highlands, and it was Stewart who set the criterion as to what the true Highland character should be. Not only had he a high standard and high ideals, but he lived up to them. Scotland has produced no finer patriot. He was shrewd yet simple, brave but kind, enthusiastic but sane. He had great feeling of understanding for others, which made him the idol of the men who served under him. And this magnetic influence over his fellows was always used for the good of his native land – the land he loved so well and of which he was so faithful a servant'.[202]

Sources

Unless otherwise stated *Sketches* refers to *Sketches of the Character, Manners, and Present State of the Highlanders of Scotland with details of the Military Service of the Highland Regiments* 3rd edition, published by Constable in 1825.

Transcripts refers to SRO (Scottish Record Office) GD1/53. 'David Stewart of Garth. 1772–1829 Transcripts and extracts of correspondence etc.' This also contains transcribed material noted as being in Macgregor Manuscripts, the Charter Room of Blair Castle etc. Otherwise the originals are in the author's possession.

1. *Sketches* 1.222.
2. *Book of Garth & Fortingall*, Northern Counties 1888. p.235.
3. SRO GD1/53. Progress of Writes of Drummacharry.
4. *Chronicles of Atholl & Tullibardine (Athol Chrons)* arranged by 7th Duke of Atholl 1908. Vol 1.458.
5. *Atholl in the Rebellion of 1745* by James Irvine Robertson. ABC Comment/Heartland. 1994.
6. SRO GD1/53. Kynachan transcripts. 7.6.1760 Indenture of Robert Stewart as law apprentice.
7. *Atholl Chrons* 1.286.
8. SRO GD1/53. Kynachan transcripts. 17.5.1718 Obligement Atholl.
9. *Atholl Chrons* 3.14.
10. *Book of Garth and Fortingall*. p.233.
11. *Sketches* 1.143.
12. Transcripts. David Stewart (DS) to Alexander Irvine (AI). 20.11.1821.
13. *Atholl Chrons* 4.147.
14. *Family and Genealogical Sketches* by Thos Sinton. Northern Counties 1911.
15. 'The Proposed Memorial to General Stewart of Garth.' *Northern Chronicle*. 11.5.1898.
16. *Atholl Chrons* 4.86.
17. Transcripts. DS to AI 17.3.1824.
18. MS Journal of Ensign Stewart, 68th Reg. The Stewart Society.
19. Transcripts. Gen Murray to Robert Stewart of Garth. 24.3.1783.

20. *Sketches* 1.416.
21. *Sketches* 1.419.
22. *Sketches* 1.426.
23. *Sketches* 1.441.
24. Transcripts. Memorandum of the Military service of Colonel David Stewart C.B. 18.7.1823.
25. Transcripts. DS to Robert Stewart of Garth 16.5.1796.
26. Transcripts. DS to Robert Stewart of Garth 26.6.1796.
27. *Sketches* 1.448.
28. Transcripts. DS to Robert Stewart of Garth 10.9.1796.
29. *Atholl Chrons* 4.159 et seq.
30. *Sketches* 1.460 et seq.
31. List of 42nd personnel receiving prize money. 8.1.1801. Black Watch Museum, Perth.
32. Transcripts. Part letter DS to Jessie Stewart. 1801.
33. Transcripts. DS will. 3.3.1801.
34. *A Biographical Dictionary of Eminent Scotsmen.* Blackie and Son. London 1869.
35. NLS (National Library of Scotland) MS 3781, f.27v. Copy of elegy for Stewart (1829).
36. *Sketches* 1.519. Transcripts. 5.10.1803 et seq.
37. Transcripts. Memorandum of the Military service of Colonel David Stewart C.B. 18.7.1823.
38. *Reminiscences and Reflections of an Octogenarian Highlander* by Duncan Campbell. Northern Counties 1910. p.287.
39. *Sketches* 2.328.
40. *Sketches* 1.321.
41. Transcripts. Memorandum regarding the Battle of Maida 14th July 1828.
42. Transcripts. Memorandum of the Military service of Colonel David Stewart of Garth C.B.
43. Transcripts. Private Memorandum. 12.7.1828.
44. *The King's Jaunt* by John Prebble. Collins 1968. p.35.
45. 'The Proposed Memorial to General Stewart of Garth.' *Northern Chronicle* 11.5.1898.
46. Transcripts. Memorandum regarding the Battle of Maida 14th July 1828.
47. Transcripts. Memorandum of the Military service of Colonel David Stewart of Garth C.B.
48. Dick Papers A3933/D. DS to Robt Dick. 24.11.1809 Black Watch Museum, Perth.
49. Dick Papers A3933/D. DS to Robt Dick. 10.6.1810.
50. Dick Papers A3933/D. DS to Robt Dick. 31.1.1811.

51. *Atholl Chrons* 4.23752.
52. PRO (Public Record Office) CO 253/25 35545 31.10.1828.
53. *Sketches* 2.406.
54. Transcripts. Hislop to DS 6.6.1811.
55. PRO WO1/116 pp.179, 183, 197, 314.
56. Transcripts. Duchess of Atholl to DS 9.10.1812.
57. Blair Castle Box 11.48. Woodford to duke. Sept 1812.
58. Transcripts. DS to AI. Drumcharry 3.1813.
59. *Sketches* Appendix cc p.188.
60. Transcripts. DS to Duncan Robertson 14.2.1814.
61. *Book of Garth and Fortingall* p.247; *Octogenarian Highlander* p.287.
62. Transcripts. DS to Duncan Robertson 14.2.1814.
63. Blair Castle Box 68.4.79. DS to Duke. 11.4.1814.
64. *Sketches* 2.54.
65. Transcripts. DS to Patrick Robertson 8.7.1814.
66. Blair Castle Box 48 Bundle 11. 257. DS to Duke 15.10.1814.
67. NLS Dep 2658 Highland Soc of London Minutes. 19.2.1814.
68. Stewarts of the South. MS. The Stewart Society.
69. NLS MS 3881.IR 18.1.1811. DS to Walter Scott.
70. Letters of Andrew Robertson. From DS. 22.1.1815.
71. Central Region Archive. McGregor of MacGregor MSS 31, 64, 68, 87, 109.
72. Transcripts. DS from Col Robertson of Struan 18.1.1815.
73. Transcripts. DS from Arch McNab 14.2.1815.
74. Transcripts. DS from Dr Alex Stewart 30.1.1816.
75. Transcripts. DS from Ld Ogilvie 8.1.1816.
76. Transcripts. DS from Col Robertson of Struan 5.12.1815.
77. Transcripts. DS from A. Campbell 16.2.1816.
78. Transcripts. DS from Macdonell of Glengarry 22.2.1816.
79. Transcripts. DS from Jas Hamilton 2.5.1816.
80. Diary of James Robertson. Transcribed by JB Loudon. Orkney Archives.
81. NLS MS 3781, f.27v.
82. Transcripts. DS from Jas Hamilton 27.2.1816.
83. Transcripts. DS from Jas Hamilton 4.3.1816.
84. *Sketches* 2.67.
85. Transcripts. DS from J Farquharson of Invercauld 17.8.1816.
86. *Sketches* 1.506.
87. Transcripts. DS from Col James Stewart of Urrard 19.3.1816.
88. *Sketches* 2. Appendix G 41.
89. *Sketches* 1.447.
90. Notebook in author's possession.
91. DS from Ld Kinnoull 15.10 1816.

92. *Memoirs of a Highland Lady* Vol 2. Canongate Classics 1992. pp.78–9.
93. Transcripts. DS to AI 27.4.1817.
94. Blair Castle Box 68.9.377. DS to duke. 19.10.1819.
95. McGregor of Macgregor MSS. DS to Sir J. Macgregor 27.3.1820.
96. McGregor of Macgregor MSS. DS to Sir J. Macgregor 19.4.1820.
97. *Atholl Chrons* 4.287.
98. McGregor of Macgregor MSS. DS to Sir J. Macgregor 30.4.1820.
99. McGregor of Macgregor MSS. DS to Sir J. Macgregor 9.5.1820.
100. Sketches of the Antiquities and Local Scenery of Fortingall. MS in author's possession.
101. *Reminiscences of my Life in the Highlands* by Joseph Mitchell. David & Charles. Reprints 1971. Vol 1.124.
102. Blair Castle Box 68.1.238/249. DS to Ld Jas Murray 22.10.1819.
103. Sophia Robertson to Capt Duncan Robertson 29th July 1818.
104. *Octogenarian Highlander* p.45.
105. McGregor of Macgregor MSS. DS to Sir J. Macgregor 5.7.1820.
106. Transcripts. DS to AI. 13.5.1820.
107. Transcripts. DS to AI. No date.
108. Transcripts. DS to AI. 26.10.1820.
109. Transcripts. DS to AI. 26.12.1820.
110. *A History of the Highland Clearances* by Eric Richards 1985.
111. SRO GD1/53 transcript of Garth & Kynachan Rent Book.
112. Transcripts. DS to AI. 'Wed. 4 o'clock'.
113. Transcripts. DS to AI. No date.
114. *Sketches* 1.92.
115. Sotheby Catalogue 9153 2.7.1980, Lot 140.
116. Transcripts. DS to AI 17.7.1821.
117. Transcripts. Copy letter to Mr Jno Stewart from A R Irvine. 30.7.1827.
118. *The Stewarts* (Vol XIX. No 2) 1993 p.83.
119. Sophia Robertson to Capt Duncan Robertson 30.7.1823. In author's possession.
120. Transcripts. Funeral Account 1823.
121. *Sketches* 1.155.
122. Transcripts. DS to AI 28.11 1821.
123. Dick Papers A3933/D. DS to Robt Dick 2.11.1818.
124. *Memorials of a Highland Lady* Vol 1.262.
125. Transcripts. Statement of Claims. 1835.
126. *The Stewarts* Stewart Society Vol XIX. No 2 1993 p.83.
127. Transcripts. DS to AI. No date.
128. Transcripts. DS to AI. 8.3.1821.
129. Transcripts. DS to AI. 'Saturday'.

130. *Tales of Whisky and Smuggling* by Stuart McHardy, p.7. Lochar Publishing 1991.
131. Blair Castle Box 68.14.4 James Findlater to Frederick Graham. 2.7.1824.
132. Transcripts. DS to AI. 7.1.1821.
133. Transcripts. DS to AI. 22.6.1821.
134. Transcripts. DS to AI. 28.11.1821.
135. Transcripts. AI to DS. 9.11.1821.
136. Sophia Robertson to Duncan Robertson. 3.9.1821.
137. Transcripts. DS to AI. 1.4.1821.
138. Transcripts. DS to AI. 9.4.1821.
139. NLS MS 791. From Constable to DS. 17.11.1820.
140. NLS MS 791. From Constable to DS. 27.12.1820.
141. NLS MS 791. From Constable to DS. 9.8.1821.
142. James Robertson to Duncan Robertson 5.1.1822. In author's possession.
143. *A Journey to the Western Isles* Oxford Standard Authors 1965 p.79.
144. *Sketches* 1.137.
145. *Sketches* 1.149.
146. *Sketches* 1.239.
147. *Sketches* 2.340.
148. *Sketches* 2.418.
149. *Sketches* 2.529.
150. *Sketches* 2.527.
151. *Sketches* 1st edition. 1.157.
152. *A History of the Highland Clearances* by Eric Richards 1985. Vol 2. 403.
153. Transcripts. DS to AI. 11.4.1822.
154. Mudie, Robert, *A Historical Account of His Majesty's Visit to Scotland* Edinburgh 1822.
155. Transcripts. DS to Jessie Irvine 25.5.1829.
156. *Octogenarian Highlander* p.43.
157. *Sketches* 1.189.
158. *L'impartial* 26.12.1829 Vol V – No 49.
159. *Memoirs of the Life of Sir Walter Scott, Bart* by John Lockhart. 2nd edition Vol 7 p.64.
160. *The King's Jaunt* by John Prebble. Collins. 1988 p.334.
161. NLS MS 3895. DS to Walter Scott 9.10.1823.
162. Transcripts. J Gordon to DS 24.2.1823.
163. Transcripts. Wm, D of Clarence to DS 8.12.1822.
164. *Sketches* 1.75
165. Transcripts. Four letters from Lady Gwydir 21.11.1822 *et seq*.
166. Transcripts. DS to AI. 14.5.1823.

167. Sophia Robertson to Duncan Robertson 30.7.1822. In author's possession.
168. *The Stewarts* (Volume XX No.1) 1996 p.10.
169. Blair Castle Bundle 14. 44. DS to Factor Graham. 1.3.1824.
170. *Reminiscences of my Life in the Highlands*, by Joseph Mitchell. David & Charles Reprints 1971. vol 1. 116
171. *The Scottish Fiddle Music Index* edited by Charles Gore. The Amazing Publishing House Ltd. 1994
172. NLS MS 591. 1856. DS to Mrs Brown 26.3.1826.
173. SRO GD1/53. Observation of the state of the roads and communications to Kenmore and Breadalbane etc. Transcribed by Roger Sylvester.
174. Transcripts. Wm Stewart of Ardvorlich to DS. 20.7.1824.
175. *Octogenarian Highlander* p.44.
176. NLS MS 9947. DS to Sir Neil Menzies. 9.3.1824.
177. *Clan Donnachaidh Annual* 1997 p.17.
178. NLS acc no 3184.
179. NLS MS 740 f.22. DS to James Smith. 8.11.1827.
180. *Sketches* 1. app FF ix.
181. Transcripts. DS to Jessie Irvine. 25.6.1827.
182. Transcripts. DS to Jessie Irvine. 1.12.1828.
183. *Atholl Chrons* 4.375.
184. PRO B 11/1748.
185. CO 253/25.35545. 31.10.1828.
186. NLS MS 3907. DS to Walter Scott. 6.10.1828.
187. Facsimile. *Sunday Dispatch* 16.2.1936.
188. Transcripts. No date.
189. NLS MS 3700. DS to James Browne adv & Mrs Browne 8.12.1828.
190. CO 253/26 35545. 10.3.1829.
191. Transcripts. Sir George Murray to DS. 24.4.1829.
192. Transcripts. DS to Jessie Irvine. 25.5.1829.
193. Transcripts. Sir George Murray to DS. 15.7.1829.
194. CO 253/26 35545. DS to Sir George Murray. 23.7.1829.
195. CO 253/26 35545. 31.7.1829.
196. CO 253/26 35545. 27.9.1829.
197. CO 253/26 35545. 29.9.1829.
198. Transcripts. J D Blythe to Jessie Irvine. 2.1.1830.
199. Transcripts. John Stewart to Jessie Irvine. 25.1.1830.
200. *Gentleman's Magazine*. March 1830.
201. Letter VI to the *Edinburgh Weekly Chronicle*. 'Destitution in Sutherlandshire'.
202. *Perthshire Advertiser* 1.7.1925.

Index

Abercromby family 42
Abercromby, Gen Sir Ralph 23, 25, 26–8, 33, 36, 37, 41–2
Aberfeldy 159, 184
Aboukir Bay 37
Alexandria, Battle of 36–42, 66, 83
Amulree 62
Andersons (tenants) 103; John 118–20
Appin of Dull 7
Arbuthnott, Sir William, Lord Provost of Edinburgh 144
Argyll, Duke of 79, 143
Atholl, District of 8, 34, 89, 154
Atholl, 4th Duke of 12; letter, 34, 46, 60, 66, 67–71; DS petition, 87–9; clearing, 92, 97–100; on *Sketches*, 137, 133, 144, 149, 154
Atholl, 8th Duke of 187
Atholl, Duchess of 60, 142
Atholemen, Association of 162

Badenoch 74
Baird, Sir David 146
Balnacraig, estate farm 112, 115
Balnarn, estate farm 115
Barbados 24, 33, 54, 71
Bathurst, Earl, Colonial Secretary 61, 70, 88
Bathurst, Honble Mr 66
Birnam 7, 110, 153
Blair Atholl 185
Blair Castle 10, 34
Blythe, J.D., Secretary to DS, 2–3, 176

Breadalbane, earls of 5, 9, 72, 92, 137; road dispute 159–162
Bridge of Tilt 163
Bruar 163

Caledonian Asylum 72
Cameron, James, riot leader 34
Campbell of Ava, Sir Archibald 183
Campbells of Glenlyon 9, 93, 183
Campbell, Alexander, musician, 78
Campbell, Duncan, author 102,
Campbell, William, composer 158
Caw, John, Provost of Perth 45–6
Celtic Society 90, 94, 136
Chalmers, Dr Thomas 166
Clarence, Duke of 151, 153, 174
Clearances 20, 63, 79, 80, 126, 131, 154
Comrie castle 7; bridge 159
Constable, Archibald, publisher 124, 152
Coshieville 8, 37
Crieff 158
Culloden 9, 10, 13–4, 38

Dalguise 89
Dalhousie, Lord 151
Dick, Maj-Gen Sir Robert 56, 59, 82, 111, 154
Drummond Hill 5, 6
Drumcharry House 6, 8, 17, 46, 109, 157, 183
Drumcharry, land of 92; descripton, 102; population, 111; debt upon 123

Dull 116
Dull, Appin of 7
Dunan 110
Duneaves 91, 93, 162
Dunkeld 7, 10, 12, 60, 62, 87, 92, 110

Edinburgh 82, 87, 135; King's Jaunt 150

Farquharson of Invercauld 83
Ferguson, Sir Adam 147
Findlater, James, Atholl factor 117
Fort George 45
Fortingall 5; description 9; disturbance in church 16; school 34, 47, 92, 97, 102; population, 166, 183
Foss 156, 166
Fraser, Capt Simon 76

Galt, John 72
Garth Castle 7, 10, 103, 118
Garth, lands of 8, 43, 100, 103 et seq.
Garth Estate, Trinidad 107
George IV 134 et seq.
Glasgow 31, 165, 184
Glen Goulandie 8, 10
Glen Lyon 5, 9, 64, 156, 167
Glengarry (in Atholl) 89; see also Macdonell of Glengarry
Glenorchy, Lord 160–2
Gow, John & Andrew, musicians 158
Gow, Nathaniel, musician 143
Gow, Niel, musician 6, 158
Graham, Frederick, Atholl factor 89, 115, 117
Grant of Rothiemurchus, Elizabeth 87, 111
Grenada 69, 71, 107

Guadeloupe 56
Gwydir, Lady, chief of Drummonds 137, 152

haberdasher's bill 157, 164
Hamilton, Capt James, Sec of Highland Soc of London 72, 76, 80, 81
Highland Society of London 43, 64, 71, 80–81, 135
Hislop, Sir Thos, Governor of Trinidad 60
Hogg, James, author 78
Home, John, author 151

Inchgarth 8, 12, 102–3, 183
Innerwick 156
Inver 62, 89
Irvine, Rev Alexander DD, brother-in-law of DS 46, 44, 62, 63; literary ambitions, 87, 77, 82, 86, 95–9, 105, 115, 120; complaint of treatment 156; death 164
Irvine, Rev Alexander DD (Sandy), nephew of DS 77, 108, 112, 184–5
Irvine, Clementina 165, 184
Irvine, David 165, 184
Irvine, Mrs Jessie see Jessie Stewart
Irvine, Robert 165, 183
Irvine, Dr William 109, 165, 184
Irvines, tenants, 103; Duncan 118 et seq.
Izett, Mrs Chalmers of Kinnaird 64

Keltneyburn 5, 50, 156, 187
Kenmore 116, 159
Kinloch Rannoch 44, 75, 166
Kinnoull, Earl of 86
Kynachan 10, 14, 79, 95, 100, 105, 115

Index

Lennox, Gen Lord George 18
Leopold, Prince 92, 153
Linnean Society 59
Litigan, estate farm 118 *et seq.*
Little Dunkeld 62, 156, 158
Lloyds, Patriotic Fund 54
Loch, James, factor to Lord Stafford 80, 98, 94
Lochaber 69
Logierait 110, 135
Lyon, Sir James, Gov of Windward Islands 182

Macara, Lt Col Robert, CO 42nd Reg. 7, 67, 82
McDiarmid, Charles of Bohally 119, 184
Macdonell of Glengarry, Alexander 74, 78, 89, 136, 139, 146, 150, 169
Macdonell of Glengarry, Gen Sir James 49, 171
McDonald, Malcolm, composer 158
McDougalls (tenants) 104, 115
MacGregor, Duncan the Piper 93, 135, 161
MacGregor-Murray, Sir John 88, 90, 94 131
McGrigor, Mr Robertson 26
McIntyre, Neil, Fortingall schoolmaster 16
Mackenzie of Gruinard, William 136, 138
MacKerchar, Duncan, musician 158
Mackid, Robert 130
MacLeod, Donald, Strathnaver 185
McLeod, Lt-Col Patrick, CO 2/78th 49
McNab of McNab, Archibald 76
Maida, Battle of 49 *et seq.*, 126, 163
Menzies, Sir John 34

Menzies, Sir Neil 75, 92, 117, 159, 161, 183
Middlesex 23
Militia Act 33, 42
Minotaur 24, 36
Mitchell, Joseph, road engineer 92, 157, 160
Moore, General Sir John 24, 48, 52
Moulin 109
Murray, Lady Elizabeth 88
Murray, Sir George, Colonial Secretary 171, 176–7
Murray, Lord George 10, 15
Murray, Col James, 77th Foot 17, 19
Murray, Lord James 58, 55, 92

Norton, Caroline, novelist 186

Ogilvie of Airlie, Lord 77
Over Blairish, estate farm 103, 116

Perth 31, 45, 110, 112
Pitlochry 109, 185
Prebble, John 53, 148
Proudfoot, Sandie, carrier 53

Raeburn, Sir Henry 71, 108, 141
Rannoch, district and loch 75, 102,
Reay, Lord 81
Regiments
    27th 47
    31st 25
    42nd 16, 20, 25; St Lucia 36; Egypt, review 41; Edinburgh parade 82; 'eagle' dispute 83
    35th 32, 182
    77th 17; mutiny 18
    78th 46 *et seq.*
    81st 52
    88th 64

93rd 63
94th 111, 184
Athole Highlanders (1813) 62
Royal West India Rangers 54
St John's Regiment of Militia 107
Robertson of Kindrochet, Capt Duncan 64, 147, 177
Robertson of Kindrochet, Mrs Sophia, née Stewart 65, 109, 122, 155, 116, 145
Robertson of Struan, Col Alexander 75, 77
Robertson of Struan, Capt 93, 162
Robertson, Dr Alexander 76
Robertson, Andrew, miniaturist 73, 75, 81
Robertson, James, diarist 79, 125
Rotmell 89, 100

St Lucia 1, 25, 80, 171 *et seq.*
St Vincent 26; fertility 30, 69
Schiehallion 11
Scott, Sir Walter 73, 78, 82, 84, 72, 77, 79, 133, 135 *et seq.*; King's Jaunt 150; letter 172–3
Scrymgeour, J M, painter 186
Sellar, Patrick, factor to Lord Stafford 99, 123–4, 130
Shand, Jimmy, musician 6
Sinclair, Sir John 72
Slavery 34, 65, 176 *et seq.*
Stafford, Marquis of 80
Stafford, Lady 80, 81, 98–9, 130, 136, 153
Stephen, James MP, abolitionist 70–1
Stewart, William of Ardvorlich 109, 137, 160
Stewarts of Ballechin 10, 90
Stewart of Bohally, Charles 16
Stewart of Urrard, Col James 83
Stewart, Col Alexander 76, 167–9
Stewart, Alexander, bastard son of *Fear Ghart* 111, 184
Stewart, Ann, bastard of John Stewart 108, 185
Stewart, Charles, Athole Highlanders (77th) 17
Stewart, Clementina, sister of DS 7, 35, 46, 64, 71, 109, 135, 141, 157; death 176
Stewart, Major-General David CB death 6; statue 14–17; boyhood 19; commission 23; Flanders 24; West Indies voyage 25; St Lucia 26; St Vincent *et seq.* 35; Mediterranean 38; Battle of Alexandria 46; reprimand & majority 48 *et seq.*; Maida 54; presentation of sword 54; West Indies 50; C-in-C Trinidad 61; Scotland 66; France 67; col & half pay 67; petition to duke 74; tartan collecting 84; Black Watch parade 87; writing *Sketches* 92; attends Taymouth gathering 97–9; Duke's opinion on *Sketches* 101; estate management 106; financial problems 110; on marriage 111; his bastards 115; estate changes 115; on emigration; further debts 117, 118 *et seq.*; problems with tenants 124; *Sketches* publication 135 *et seq.*; King's Jaunt 148; importance in establishing Highland image 152; marriage plans 158; road improvements 166; new churches 168; legacy 171; Governor's appointment 176; St Lucia 181; statue 187
Stewart, Capt James, factor to Atholl 89

Stewart, Jean, bastard of DS 111
Stewart, Jessie, sister of DS 7, 36, 46, 57, 109, 165, 167, 174, 183; death 185
Stewart, John, brother of DS 7, 30, 35, 107 *et seq.*, 182, 183
Stewart, Neil, Montgomeries Highlanders 17
Stewart, Neil, bastard son of DS 112–13
Stewart, Robert (*Fear Ghart*), father of DS 7–13, 17–20, 25, 28, 46, 63, 93; stroke, 101, 111; death 120; DS's opinion on 121
Stewart, Robert (Robbie Uncle) 9–10, 11, 93
Stewart, William, elder brother of DS 7, 13, 16, 34; Militia riots 56, 93, 94–6; child 111; death 114
Stirling Castle 19
Strathbraan 62

Strathfillan Society 131, 153
Strathtay 7, 34, 43, 92, 98, 105
Stuart, Sir John, C-in-C Sicily 49, 51
Sutherland, Countess of *see* Lady Stafford
Sutherland 18, 75, 83, 93, 98, 126
Sword, silver-hilted 54

Tay Bridge 157–8
Taymouth Castle 87, 131, 159
Trinidad 31, 52–3, 53–56, 69 *et seq.*
True Highlanders, Society of 74, 78, 131
Tulliemet 89
Tummel Bridge 10, 13, 117, 157–8
Tynadalloch 106, 156

Weem 6, 36, 158, 151
Wilberforce, William 70
Woodford, Sir Ralph 60–1, 70

York, Duke of 23, 43, 46, 45, 83